Corporate Investment Decisions

Corporate Investment Decisions

Principles and Practice

Michael Pogue

Corporate Investment Decisions: Principles and Practice
Copyright © Business Expert Press, LLC, 2010.

First published in 2010 by
Business Expert Press, LLC
222 East 46th Street, New York, NY 10017
www.businessexpertpress.com

ISBN-13: 978-1-60649-064-8 (paperback)
ISBN-10: 1-60649-064-4 (paperback)

ISBN-13: 978-1-60649-065-5 (e-book)
ISBN-10: 1-60649-065-6 (e-book)

DOI 10.4128/9781606490655

A publication in the Business Expert Press Managerial Accounting collection

Collection ISSN: 2152-7113 (print)
Collection ISSN: 2152-7121 (electronic)

Cover design by Jonathan Pennell
Interior design by Scribe, Inc.

First edition: July 2010

10 9 8 7 6 5 4 3 2 1

Printed in Taiwan

For Aileen and my son Ryan

Abstract

In these turbulent financial and economic times, the importance of sound investment decisions becomes a critical variable in underpinning future business success and, indeed, survival. The difficulties currently encountered globally by firms in both raising finance and making predictions concerning the future economic environment raise the already prominent role of capital budgeting in the arena of financial decision making.

This book is intended for both practicing managers who require a thorough knowledge of the principles of making investment decisions in the real world and for students undertaking financial courses, whether at undergraduate, MBA, or professional levels.

The subject matter encompasses relevant aspects of the investment decision, varying from a basic introduction, to the appraisal techniques available, to placing investment decisions within both strategic and international contexts, and coverage of recent developments including real options, value at risk, and environmental investments.

Keywords

Capital expenditure, appraisal techniques, risk, strategic investment decisions, international capital budgeting, recent developments

Contents

Acknowledgments

Thanks to UNCTAD for free permission to reproduce figures 9.1. and 9.2 from the UNCTAD World Investment Report 2008.

Thanks to Ken Merchant and David Parker for the opportunity to make this book a reality and to Cindy Durand for her advice and encouragement in completing the manuscript.

Introduction

The historically low interest rates in the current economic climate would appear to provide an ideal scenario for companies to invest long term in value-creating capital expenditures. However, the combination of declining corporate profitability together with significant ongoing difficulties in raising external finance continues to exert downward pressure upon the funds available for investment. Almost daily, corporate announcements include a statement regarding an intention to significantly reduce capital expenditure (hereafter capex) during the upcoming financial year. The following sample of recent financial disclosures from the automobile, telecommunication, and mining sectors are indicative of the current trend:

> Toyota Motor Corp will slash capital and research spending for a second year in a move that threatens to erode a significant advantage it holds over ailing U.S. based rivals. Toyota said Friday its budget for this financial year will cut capital spending by more than a third, to $8 billion from $13 billion. GM last year said it would cut capital spending to $4.8 billion in 2009 and 2010, down from $9 billion.[1]

> AT&T, the largest U.S. telecoms group, yesterday said it would cut capital spending by 10 to 15 per cent this year from the $19.7bn it spent in 2008.[2]

> Anglo American Plc has completed a wide ranging review of its capital expenditure programme in recent weeks, at a time when the mining industry has experienced an unprecedented period of rapid declines in commodity prices due to global economic uncertainty. Capital expenditure has been capped at $4.5 billion, a reduction of more than 50%.[3]

The large capex cuts announced by aluminum giants are reducing the number and size of greenfield smelters that were coming on stream in the coming years. Rio Tinto Alcan is considering slashing its capex for 2009 from $9bn to $4bn. The company has not given details on which projects will be axed, but revealed that some projects will be delayed and others cancelled altogether.[4]

A more general overview is provided by the following excerpt from Reuters:

A trade group for lenders that finance half the capital equipment investment in the United States told Reuters on Monday that businesses postponed new capex spending once again in June as underwriting standards continued to tighten. The Equipment Leasing and Finance Association, which measures the overall volume of financings used to fund equipment acquisitions, fell 36.9% year-over-year in June to $5.2 billion.[5]

Despite the apparently foreboding economic outlook, at least in the short term, it remains critical that companies appreciate the importance of capex and continue to prioritize spending in spite of declining profitability and competing demands from, inter alia, dividends and pension contributions. Investments are important not only for companies attempting to achieve an optimal asset structure but also for enabling the introduction of new products or achieving structural cost reductions.

In addition to recognizing that investment is a prerequisite for both growth and survival at the corporate level, it is also clear that national economic growth is strongly correlated with investment intensity, especially for emerging economies. On average, about 20% of world gross domestic product is spent on capital investment, with 8 of the 10 fastest growing economies exhibiting investment intensities significantly in excess of the average.

However, while actively encouraging capital investment, we must also recognize the complexities associated with identifying, evaluating, and implementing appropriate investment strategies. Finance textbooks generally propose a primary corporate objective of maximizing shareholder wealth and then proceed to suggest that this is achieved simply by investing in value-creating projects (i.e., those having positive net present value). An overarching assumption commonly made is that of a perfect capital market, which, in turn, assumes a world of perfect information, devoid of uncertainty (along with various other associated assumptions). Decision makers currently operate in a world radically different from that of the finance textbook, where high levels of volatility are being experienced in consumer, commodity, and financial markets, and even short-term predictions are not made with any degree of confidence. Against this backdrop, the uncertainty inherent in real-world investment decisions, which necessitate a medium- to long-term perspective to be taken in normal circumstances, increases significantly, and the information required to evaluate potential investment projects becomes almost impossible to forecast.

In addition to the uncertainties inherent in forecasting the prospective returns from potential investments, a myriad of other difficulties face those responsible for investment decisions. Investment patterns are heavily influenced by the industrial sector, within which the companies operating in transport, telecommunications, oil and gas, and utilities are among the most capital intensive. The rate of technological change is also significant in particular industry sectors, with companies encountering timing issues when determining when to make the transition to a new technology. While no company can afford to ignore technological developments, there can also be significant risks from moving too early and encountering technological challenges that could prove insurmountable. When observing the bigger picture, it is also clear that cyclicality in economic systems occurs in a regular, though not predictable, pattern. Companies tend to react, though not immediately, to such imbalances between demand and supply. Longer delays increase the susceptibility of the economic cycle to cyclical patterns, so quicker responses can reduce a company's dependence on economic cycles and also allow it to gain an advantage over its competitors.

Given the complexities of the real world in which companies operate, it becomes transparent that no textbook can provide a panacea to all the problems faced by those responsible for making investment decisions. However, despite this assertion, the existence of logical and consistent procedures can prove beneficial when attempting to identify and evaluate long-term projects. While recognizing that practical investment decisions could be deemed to be "as much art as science," and sophisticated valuation techniques cannot be viewed as a substitute for intuition and experience, the primary objective of this book is to provide an appropriate combination of theory and practice. In the pursuit of this objective, it is intended that the content will be of relevance not only to those studying investment appraisal as a component of an academic or professional course but also to those practitioners who may be encountering the vagaries of assessing investment projects.

The opening chapter of the text provides both an overview of the financial environment in which businesses operate and also an assessment of the significance of the investment decision within the overall financial management function. Subsequently, in chapter 2 we develop a framework with the intention of describing a logical sequence of stages through which a typical investment proposal may pass, commencing with the identification of the investment opportunity and concluding with an assessment of the postimplementation performance of the chosen projects. Investment decisions can be considerably enriched by the experience and intuition of the managers involved. Given our assertion that the process of making investment decisions is "as much art as science," we can benefit from analyzing the outcome of decisions made previously.

Chapter 3 describes and evaluates the basic appraisal techniques that are commonly applied to the estimated profits, or cash flows, predicted for a potential investment. Some of the shortcomings of the basic techniques are then addressed by considering modified versions of these techniques. Finally, survey evidence of the techniques used in practice is discussed and critically compared with the recommendations emanating from academia.

Chapters 4 and 5 consider the adjustments necessary for cash flows to reflect the respective impacts of taxation, inflation, and risk and uncertainty. Initially in chapter 4, taxation is considered with reference to tax depreciation allowances and corporate taxation payable on the projected profits generated by the proposal. Subsequently, the issues raised by the presence of inflation are considered together with the influence on both cash flows and discount rates.

Chapter 5 is devoted to the treatment of risk and uncertainty, a fundamental problem in investment decisions due to their implicitly unpredictable nature. Techniques available for allowing the inclusion of risk into either the cash flow projections or the discount rate will be considered and evaluated together with evidence gathered from survey studies.

Capital rationing, a topic perhaps particularly relevant to the situation that many companies face in the current economic downturn, is addressed in chapter 6. In the perfect capital market assumed in the textbook, companies can invest unlimited amounts of capital and do not face restrictions in this regard. The implications of hard and soft capital rationing are also discussed, and the appropriate techniques for dealing with both single- and multiperiod capital rationing are illustrated.

In chapter 7, we consider another variant of the investment decision in which companies are faced with the problem of replacing capital assets. A range of varying time options are generally available, and the optimum replacement cycle is identified using techniques particular to this decision. Also in this chapter, we consider the lease versus buy decision that, although technically a financing decision, is a dilemma often faced particularly in smaller firms where capital available for projects is limited.

Some investments could be viewed as essential, such as the decision to replace machinery that is nearing the end of its economic life and is unlikely to have a significant impact upon current activities. In contrast, successful strategic investment decisions are likely to impinge heavily on competitive advantage and will influence what the company does, where it does it, and how it does it. We consider strategic investment decisions in chapter 8 and assess the emerging techniques to assist strategic decisions prior to examining the extent to which such techniques find application in practice.

In the modern global business environment, firms are often compelled to consider expansion into foreign markets in search of additional revenue or when faced with stagnating domestic markets. Ultimately, this may involve the establishment of a production facility in the foreign market requiring significant capital commitment and exposing the firm to additional risks surrounding, inter alia, currency fluctuations and political uncertainty. In chapter 9, we attempt to provide a brief overview of the motives underlying foreign expansion and an appreciation of the additional risk factors requiring consideration when contemplating foreign expansion.

The current frontiers of investment decision theory are discussed and evaluated in chapter 10. Although the concept of real options originated in the 1980s, real options have not appeared to be widely applied, at least in textbook form, despite the potential benefits they offer by incorporating flexibility into the investment decision. More recently, the concept of value at risk has enjoyed both popularity and some notoriety in the financial sector, and we consider the application of some of its derivatives to capital budgeting. Other developments that have their origins elsewhere but merit consideration include duration analysis (from the bond markets) and the intriguing concept of decision markets, in which an internal betting market is established and used to predict the most likely outcomes.

We conclude by attempting to provide a brief overview of the current environment for capital budgeting, in which economies are beginning to emerge from recession and firms are encountering important investment decisions involving where and when to invest. In addition, pressures are mounting for the reduction of carbon emissions, which may well culminate in legislation obliging firms to incur significant capital expenditure commitments when corporate profitability is still recovering, and the purse strings of the capital markets have yet to be loosened.

CHAPTER 1

The Financial Environment

The world economy is currently deeply mired in the most severe financial and economic crisis since the Second World War. At the end of 2008, most economies were experiencing the sharpest fall in consumer and business confidence in 20 years, on top of which, commodities had suffered their steepest decline since 1945. Despite enormous write-downs by banks in the United States and Europe, problems have not gone away and world gross product (WGP) is expected to contract by 2.6% in 2009 (3.9% in the developed economies).[1] There is little evidence of any "loosening" in the financial markets despite governments pumping billions into the banking system and, consequently, companies of all sizes struggle to acquire new financing or even maintain existing levels of borrowing. Banks not only are more selective about the clients to which they lend, but also they are charging more, and foreign banks have tended to retrench, thereby reducing borrowing facilities even further. In addition, corporate bond markets are closed to all but the best rated companies. Volatility in the financial markets means that only the most nimble of treasurers will succeed in navigating them. Moreover, lurking in the background, obscured by the difficulties of the financial markets and threatening the stability of the economic and financial systems, is the possibility of an H1N1 pandemic.

Such levels of unpredictability are providing many sleepless nights for CFOs and corporate treasurers, who are tasked with the management of their company's financial risk. Experts are now unanimous in underlining the fundamental importance of cash, as illustrated by Dev Sanyal,[2] group treasurer of British Petroleum: "cash on a balance sheet has moved from being economically inefficient, losing the spread between debt and investment, to being a vital element in the battle to maintain liquidity at times of capital market disruptions."

The role of the corporate treasurer has never been more important as the attention of company boards is dominated by risk management and cash. Moreover, even if eventual economic recovery is likely, the task of the CFO may become even more complex in predicting the rate of recovery and acquiring the financial resources required to finance growth.

A further influence on the role of the CFO has been the recent attention focused on corporate governance emanating from the accounting scandals in the United States (Enron, Worldcom) and Europe (Maxwell, Parmalat). The growing importance of stock markets and an increasingly dispersed ownership of public companies throughout the world have promoted an increasing governmental interest in shareholder protection and better standards of corporate governance. As a consequence, legislation has been enacted in the form of the Sarbanes-Oxley Act (SOX) in the United States and the Combined Code in the United Kingdom. The regulatory frameworks already adopted in the United States and the United Kingdom have increasingly become the model for systems evolving in other countries. Financial managers are the principal agents for ensuring compliance with these systems.

The Financial Decisions

Every decision made in business has financial implications, and any decision that involves the use of money is a financial decision. When making financial decisions, conventional corporate financial theory assumes that the unifying objective is to maximize the value of the business or firm, often referred to as maximizing shareholder wealth. Some critics would argue against the choice of a single objective and argue that firms should have multiple objectives that accommodate various associated stakeholders. Others would recommend a focus on simpler and more direct objectives, such as market share or profitability, or, in the current economic climate, simply surviving may assume priority.

If the main objective in corporate finance is to maximize company value, any financial decision that increases the value of a company is considered good, whereas one that reduces value is deemed poor. It follows that company value must be determined by the three primary financial decisions—financing, investment, and dividend—and recognizing that the value of a company is determined primarily by the present value of its expected cash flows. Investors form expectations concerning such future cash flows based on observable current cash flows and expected future growth and value the company accordingly. However, this seemingly simple formulation of value is tested by both the interactions between the financial decisions and conflicts of interest that emerge among the stakeholders (managers, shareholders, and lenders).

The Financing Decision

All companies, irrespective of size or complexity, are ultimately financed by a mix of borrowed money (debt) and owners' funds (equity). The main issues to be considered are the availability and suitability of the various sources of finance and whether the existing mix of debt and equity is appropriate. Debt finance is generally regarded as cheaper than equity due to lower issue costs and tax benefits, but it raises considerations of financial risk. In contrast, equity finance is more expensive, but the financial markets tend, on average, to react negatively to equity issues. In both the United States and the United Kingdom, companies tend to rely heavily on retained earnings as a source of finance in accordance with pecking order theory, which suggests that companies both avoid external financing when internal financing is available and avoid new equity financing when new debt financing can be sourced at reasonable cost.

Once the optimal financing mix has been determined, the duration of the financing can be addressed, with the recommendation being that this should match the duration of the assets being financed. However, companies may elect to finance aggressively (using short-term finance to finance longer term assets) or defensively (matching long-term finance with shorter term assets), depending on cost and risk considerations.

The efficient capital markets hypothesis concludes that a stock market is efficient if the market price of a company's securities correctly reflects all relevant information. In particular, share prices can be relied on to reflect the true economic worth of the shares. This would imply that attempting to time the issuance of new financing is a futile exercise.

The Investment Decision

In its simplest form, an investment decision can be defined as involving the company making a cash outlay with the aim of receiving future cash inflows. Capital investment decisions are generally long-term corporate finance decisions relating to fixed assets, and management must allocate limited resources among competing opportunities in a process known as capital budgeting. The magnitude of the investment can vary significantly from relatively small items of machinery and equipment to launching a new product line or constructing a foreign production facility. We can distinguish between the assets the company has already acquired, called assets in place, and those in which the company is expected to invest in the future, referred to as growth assets. The latter include internal and external development projects, such as investing in new technologies or entering into joint ventures, thereby potentially creating future investment opportunities in addition to generating benefits from current use. As we shall see, such investments present particular managerial and valuation difficulties, as traditional valuation and capital budgeting techniques are both difficult to apply and may lead to incorrect conclusions.

Projects that pass through the preliminary screening phase become candidates for rigorous financial appraisal. To assist in making investment decisions and ensure consistency, methods of investment appraisal are required that can be applied to the whole spectrum of investment decisions, and that should help to decide whether any individual investment will enhance shareholder wealth. The results of the appraisal will heavily influence the project selection for investment decisions. However, appraisal techniques should not be recognized as providing a decision guide rather than providing a definitive answer.

The investment appraisal process and ultimate decision may also be subject to agency problems arising between the owners and the manager as a result of asymmetric information. It has been suggested[3] that managers have an incentive to grow their companies beyond the optimal size and predict that agency conflicts give rise to overinvestment. A contrasting theory[4] predicts that asymmetric information between informed managers and the public market causes underinvestment.

The Dividend Decision

The dividend decision is the third major category of corporate long-term financial decision and perhaps the most elusive and controversial. As with the financing and investment decisions, the main research question is whether the pattern (not magnitude) of dividend policy can impact shareholder wealth; that is, does a particular pattern of dividends maximize shareholder wealth?

The apparently simple question facing the board of a quoted company is that of splitting the after-tax cash flows between dividend payments to the shareholders and retentions within the company. The dividend irrelevancy hypothesis[5] suggested that dividends should simply be treated as a residual after desired investments had been made. However, such a conclusion is somewhat tautological based on the range of assumptions incorporated into the analysis (perfect capital market, no taxation, no transactions costs, no flotation costs, etc.). Upon relaxation of these assumptions, there could be a marked preference for or against dividends from either the company or the shareholders. Moreover, consideration of the clientele effect and signaling placed exogenous pressure on companies to maintain their dividend payouts. Despite such pressure, the trend during recent years has been for a decreasing number of companies to pay dividends and increased popularity of share buybacks. The current economic climate continues to place further downward pressure on dividend payouts.

While we have discussed the three decisions independently, in practice they are closely linked. A company's investment, financing, and distribution decisions are necessarily interrelated by the fact that sources of cash equal uses of cash. An increase in operating cash flow could be used to increase capital expenditure. Alternatively, it could be employed to reduce debt, increase dividends, or finance any combination of investment and financing decisions. Some evidence[6] suggests that increases in cash flow are predominantly used to decrease debt and have an insignificant impact on capital investment. Similarly, a decision to increase investment can only be accommodated by either reducing dividend payments or raising additional finance. Less obviously, the source of new finance raised may influence the discount rate used in the appraisal and may impinge on the acceptance or rejection of the investment project.

What Is Capital Expenditure?

Capital expenditure is investment in the business with the objective of creating shareholder value. This additional value arises predominantly from the cash flow created by the investment, rather than the physical assets purchased. A capital expenditure arises when a company spends money to either acquire new fixed assets or enhance the value of existing fixed assets. For taxation purposes, capital expenditures are costs that cannot be deducted in the year in which they are incurred and must be capitalized in the balance sheet. Subsequently, the costs are depreciated or amortized over their useful economic life, depending on whether the assets are tangible or intangible.

A business or industry is capital intensive if it requires heavy capital investment relative to the level of sales or profits that those assets can generate. Industries generally regarded as capital intensive include oil production and refining, telecommunications, and transportation. In all of these industries, a large financial commitment is necessary just to get the first unit of goods or services produced. Once the upfront investment is made, there may be economies of scale, and the high barrier to entry tends to result in few competitors. In addition, because capital intensive companies have substantial assets to finance, they tend to borrow more heavily and gearing and interest cover ratios require more attention. The amount of capital required can sometimes be reduced by leasing or renting assets rather than purchasing them, which is particularly prevalent in the airline industry.

Capital expenditure can be analyzed in various ways, with perhaps one of the more useful classifications being into major projects, routine expenditure, and replacement expenditure.

1. Major projects generally fall within the category of strategic investment and are nonroutine investments, with significant long-term consequences for the company (see chapter 9). Their significance arises as a consequence of the commitment of substantial amounts of resources (finance, human capital, information, etc.) and, moreover, they can involve a much higher cost commitment than simply the initial investment capital. In addition, the outcome of the project will affect not only the company itself but also competitors

and the environment for an extended period of time. For example, investment in a new technology may impact the speed of innovation within the entire industry.

The more strategic the investment, the more complex and less structured the decision process will be. This arises due to both the wider impact on the company and the involvement of more people in the process, particularly management at higher levels. Senior management not only intervene in strategic investment decisions but also manipulate the decision contexts such as organizational structure, reward systems, and corporate culture.

Strategic investments can also be distinguished from more routine decisions by their broader consequences. Dynamically, they often give rise to other projects and do not end when the project is implemented. More recently, environmental investing has received prominence, with compliance with legislation and attempts to reduce carbon emissions requiring consideration on investment agendas.

2. Routine capital expenditure involves relatively small amounts of financing, is mainly inconsequential for the future of the company, and may be largely discretionary in nature. Its purpose may be to improve working conditions or expenditure on maintenance, or be competition oriented. Working conditions may be enhanced by the replacement or updating of office furniture or computer equipment and software. Maintenance expenditure would be significant for agencies responsible for transportation networks, in which investment in employee training can give a competitive edge. Decisions regarding such expenditure are not likely to be subject to a high level of formal analysis or involve the input of senior management. The discretionary nature of these decisions may mean that cost center or divisional managers are simply allocated a budget and given authority to spend up to that amount.

3. Replacement capital expenditure may be necessary for differing reasons, such as obsolescence or simply an asset reaching the end of its useful economic life. Technological advances may lead to more efficient production methods, and the investment may be analyzed on the basis of expected cost savings. Alternatively, certain assets will require replacement after extended use, and company policies may be in place to replace computers or company cars after a specific

period of time. This latter type of investment may be subject to formal analysis to determine an optimal replacement cycle (see chapter 8).

Importance of Capex

Of the three financial decisions considered, it is generally accepted that the investment decision is the most significant. Financing and dividend decisions should not be ignored, particularly in the current economic climate, but the investment decision has certain characteristics that merit particular attention.

Resource Usage

By definition, investment decisions involve expenditure, whether financed by retained earnings or by a new issue of equity shares or debt capital. Irrespective of the source of finance, companies must ensure that the optimum benefit is obtained and scarce capital is not wasted. Invariably, the amounts spent are significant and should also be monitored to avoid the common tendency to overspend. Investment projects are also typically intensive in terms of labor resources, in respect to both labor employed on implementing the project and management time spent on the decision process.

Impact on Long-Term Future

Investments, whether of a personal or corporate nature, are transacted with a goal to generating future returns. Companies invest in new product lines or new markets with the objective of generating additional sales and profits, to supplement the declining sales of existing products or traditional markets. Such investments may involve negative cash flows for several years prior to the new product or market being established. Consequently, inappropriate investments that fail to generate the expected returns will result in declining profitability and potential write-offs of the money invested. In the worst-case scenario, the future survival of the company may be endangered, and inevitably its competitive position will deteriorate.

Irreversibility

This refers to the extent to which it is possible to back out and recover expenditure on a project that has been implemented, but subsequently is proven to be an error of judgment. In general, few projects can be reversed without incurring significant cost. The degree of irreversibility is largely determined by the specificity of the investment to the particular industry. If the investment is specific to a single industry, a poor investment is unlikely to prove attractive to other companies in the same industry, thereby limiting the opportunity for disposal. However, if the project is less specific and could find an application in other industries, there is an increased possibility of interest elsewhere.

Impact on Reputation

Impact on reputation concerns the consideration of the impact of a failed venture on market confidence in the company and its overall reputation. The effect of withdrawing from one activity, or a range of activities, needs to be assessed in terms of the general impact on the remaining operations. Any company ceasing operations in one sector needs to avoid damage to its wider reputation, and any withdrawal requires careful management.

CHAPTER 2

The Appraisal Process

The finance literature tends to view the decision maker as more of a technician than an entrepreneur, with the assumption being that the application of theoretically correct appraisal techniques will result in an optimal choice of projects and, subsequently, maximization of shareholder value. Implicit in this approach is that investment ideas simply emerge; free information is readily available; projects are considered in isolation, devoid of further interactions; and qualitative factors are relatively unimportant.

In reality, managers operate in a very different environment, facing relatively unstructured, complex decisions with ambiguity and irreversibility typically present. Clearly, in such circumstances we must consider the entire decision process and not simply emphasize the formal appraisal techniques. Various theories of decision making are available, suggesting a multistage process that typically involves defining the problem, gathering information, considering alternatives, and finally implementing the decision.

Identification of Investment Opportunities

The first stage in the capital budgeting process involves the identification of investment opportunities and the generation of project proposals. Usually, the proposal should indicate how the project fits into the existing long-term strategic plan of the business, though certain projects may be capable of altering the strategic plan, thereby creating a two-way relationship.

Identification of profitable proposals will not happen automatically, and top management should encourage a culture that not only encourages but also rewards investment ideas from all levels of the organization. A structure should be in place that encourages, collects, and communicates new ideas. Ideas should be acknowledged, even if not used, as such recognition motivates creative people. Creativity and innovation are key elements in a competitive world. A recent survey[1] suggests that high-performing companies focused on small ideas, while low-performing companies tended to go after big ones. Big ideas tend to be copied by competitors, whereas it is more likely that small ideas will remain proprietary and can accumulate into a big competitive advantage, which is often sustainable.

For the identification of strategic investment opportunities, management needs to conduct environmental scanning to gather information that is mainly externally oriented. Reliance on the formal information within most organizations is not likely to be particularly productive in the identification of nonroutine investment ideas.

Preliminary Screening

The identification phase may generate a significant number of potential investment proposals, but it is not feasible or desirable to perform a rigorous project analysis of every investment idea. The purpose of the preliminary screening stage is to filter out projects deemed to be marginal or unsound, because it is not worth spending resources to thoroughly evaluate such proposals. Some ideas may not be consistent with strategic policy or may fall outside the areas identified for growth or maintenance. Other considerations addressed at this stage could include resource availability (e.g., finance), technical feasibility, and an acceptable level of risk.

The preliminary screening may involve some basic quantitative analysis and judgments relying largely on intuition and prior experience. The quality of data available at this stage is generally poor, so the application of more sophisticated financial analysis is not warranted. The simple payback method is often used to provide a crude assessment of project profitability and risk. Those projects that meet the initial screening requirements are included in an annual capital budget, though this does not provide an authorization for proceeding with the investment. In particular industries or for public sector agencies, there may be a strong environmental influence on the screening of projects.

Assessing the Alternatives

Certain proposals may be achievable via different routes. For example, the introduction of a new product line may require a substantial investment in new machinery and considerable training costs for the employees. However, the same outcome could be achieved by subcontracting the production, thereby reducing the immediate cash outflow and the potential costs associated with failure. On the other hand, existing employees may react unfavorably to subcontracting, as they may view such decisions as impacting future job security.

Project Evaluation

Projects that are successful at the preliminary screening stage become candidates for rigorous financial appraisal to assess whether they are likely to add value to the company. The project will need to be classified on the basis of its impact on the investment decision process. Projects may be independent, having minimal impact on the acceptance or rejection of other projects, or mutually exclusive, in which two or more projects cannot be pursued simultaneously. Another category is that of contingent projects, in which acceptance or rejection is dependent on the acceptance or rejection of one or more other projects.

The initial step in this phase will generally involve the prediction of the expected future cash flows of the project, along with some assessment of the risk associated with these cash flows. This step will clearly involve the application of both forecasting techniques and risk analysis while estimating the cash flows. Subsequently, the project will be subjected to one or more financial appraisal techniques, the results of which will be utilized in making the final decision on whether or not to proceed with the project.

In addition to quantitative analysis, the project will be further evaluated with regard to qualitative factors, which are difficult to assess in monetary terms. This would include societal and environmental impacts, along with potential legal difficulties. Most of these factors are externalities and, unless particularly significant, are unlikely to affect the decision regarding otherwise viable projects.

Making the Decision

The results from the financial analysis, together with consideration of qualitative factors, will then form the basis of the decision support information. Management will use this information, in conjunction with their own experience and judgment, to make a final decision regarding the acceptance or rejection of the proposal. The level of management at which the decision is made will be determined by factors that include the magnitude and strategic importance of the proposal. Division managers may have authority to make decisions regarding projects up to a specified amount, but larger projects will require upper management input and determination. Similarly, projects of a strategic nature are primarily a topic for upper management consideration.

Project Implementation and Monitoring

Projects that successfully pass through the decision stage become eligible to proceed to the implementation stage of the process. The successful delivery of the capital investment program is crucial to the company and its stakeholders, as are the implementation of effective controls and the management of associated risks. No two projects are alike; therefore, the bespoke nature requires a flexible and dynamic approach to ensure they are delivered both within budget and on time. On too many occasions, projects are affected by time or cost overruns, or fail to meet business objectives. Often, management focus is then diverted to resolving project related issues, and refinancing may prove necessary. More significantly, the implementation of strategy may be threatened and ultimately insolvency may result.

Postimplementation Audit

A successful project implementation is often viewed as the end of the process rather than a milestone. Investment decision making is a heuristic process whereby lessons can be learned for the future, and the postimplementation audit (PIA) is a vital component for continuous improvement. Useful feedback from the audit can contribute greatly to both project appraisal and strategy formulation.

In essence, a PIA should provide an objective and independent appraisal of the success of a capital expenditure project in progressing the objectives of the business as originally intended. A comparison of the actual cash flows and other expected benefits with those forecast at the time of authorization forms the basis of the audit.

A PIA is fundamentally a control device for the whole system of capital expenditure decision making and is usually initiated within the first year of the life of the project. Scrutiny of the implementation and early operation of selected investment projects may, in turn, lead to a fine-tuning of the project to steer it back on course, a significant change in the development of the project, or in the worst case, a decision to abandon the project. Potential difficulties associated with the use of PIAs include distinguishing the relevant costs and benefits of a new project from existing company activities, the cost involved in performing the audit, and significant unpredicted changes in market conditions. Moreover, the likelihood of being subject to a PIA may encourage managers to exhibit a more risk-averse attitude, which manifests itself in a reluctance to propose more innovative, but also risky, projects. The PIA should be used in a manner that does not result in managers only suggesting "safe projects." In particular, clear procedures for PIAs should be laid out, and the learning objective should be emphasized, instead of it being seen as an attempt to find scapegoats for unsuccessful projects.

Recent research[2] views the capital budgeting decision as a four stage process, namely identification, development, selection, and control, and reviews the survey literature from 1984 to 2008. It confirms the critique of other authors[3] in concluding that the selection stage, emphasizing the use of particular project evaluation techniques, dominates the survey literature over the entire period. In pointing the direction for potential future research in this area, they favor the decision support system as a fruitful and challenging survey topic, and advise that future work should avoid the assumption "that a set of well-defined capital investment opportunities, with all of the informational needs clearly specified, suddenly appears on an executive's desk and all that is needed is for the manager to [select] the project(s) with the highest expected payoff."[4] More specifically, consideration of the actual process of obtaining the required input from management to enhance existing risk assessment and adjustment models or to construct new models would appear worthy of further investigation.

CHAPTER 3

The Appraisal Techniques

Once cash flows have been estimated, the projects are then subjected to project evaluation techniques to further assess their potential for achieving the financial objectives of the company. A wide range of techniques are available, broadly divided into two groups: those that make adjustments for the time value of money (the discounted cash flow [DCF] group) and those that do not include such an adjustment (the traditional group).

In this chapter, we shall assess the basic techniques available, identifying their respective strengths and weaknesses, and then evaluate some modifications made to these techniques to overcome the identified problems. Finally, we shall address available survey evidence to examine the incidence of practical application of the various techniques.

The Traditional Techniques

This category of appraisal technique does not make any adjustment for the time value of money; that is, it treats cash flows as having similar real value irrespective of the time period in which they arise. This is often regarded as an inherent weakness of these techniques, as invariably project lives transcend a period of several years.

The two main techniques in this category are the payback period and the accounting rate of return (or return on capital employed). We shall illustrate and discuss each method in turn.

Payback Period (PB)

This is a measure of time rather than profitability, and is simply calculated as the time required for the cash inflows from a capital investment project to equal the cash outflows. As a result of its simplicity, PB is often used as an initial screening device to filter investment proposals.

Example 3.1

A company is currently considering three potential investment projects, each with a 7-year duration, and has estimated the expected cash flows shown in Table 3.1.

The payback period for each proposal is calculated by cumulating the cash inflows until the initial cash outflow is achieved. In each case, the payback period is 5 years, so all three projects would be equally attractive. The decision to accept or reject the projects would then be based on a cutoff criteria established by the company. If the required payback period was 3 years, the projects would be rejected. But if it was 5 years or more, the projects would be acceptable.

Although payback is often used for initial screening, it is not advisable for projects to be evaluated solely on the basis of payback. If a project passes the payback test, it should then be evaluated using a more sophisticated project appraisal technique. The previous example illustrates some of the weaknesses of the payback technique:

1. It ignores the timing of cash flows within the payback period as evidenced by Projects A and B. On the basis that uncertainty regarding cash flows estimates increases with time, the project that yields higher cash flows in earlier years (Project B) would usually be preferred, but this is not considered in the payback calculation.
2. It ignores the cash flows once the payback period has been reached and therefore disregards total project return. Project C has the same payback period as Projects A and B, but A and B continue to generate positive cash inflows, whereas C incurs negative cash flows.

Table 3.1. Expected Cash Flows

	Year 0	Year 1	Year 2	Year 3	Year 4	Year 5	Year 6	Year 7
Project A	(15,000)	1,000	2,000	3,000	4,000	5,000	6,000	7,500
Project B	(15,000)	5,000	4,000	3,000	2,000	1,000	3,000	4,000
Project C	(15,000)	3,000	3,000	3,000	3,000	3,000	(4,000)	(3,500)

3. The PB provides a measure of the time period taken to recoup the initial investment, but does not measure the intrinsic profitability or return from the project.

4. Perhaps the most basic criticism of PB is that no consideration is given to the time value of money, with each dollar or pound of return being treated as having equal value, irrespective of when it is obtained; that is, the cash flow in year 7 is treated as equal, in real terms, to cash flow at the commencement of the project.

Despite such criticisms, there are also some merits of calculating payback in addition to its simplicity of calculation and ease of understanding:

1. A focus on early payback may enhance liquidity and provide an estimate of when the money will be available for other projects. This may be of particular relevance when a company has limited capital resources.

2. Shorter term forecasts are likely to be more reliable, on the basis that uncertainty increases when attempting to forecast further into the future.

3. Similarly, projects with longer payback periods can be viewed as more risky, again on the basis of greater uncertainty.

Accounting Rate of Return (ARR)

The ARR calculates a percentage rate of return using average accounting profit of the project life together with the capital outlay. The latter can be expressed as either the initial outlay or the average investment over the project life. It should be noted that this technique uniquely uses accounting profit in contrast to cash flow, which is used by the other appraisal techniques. Once estimated, the ARR of the proposal is compared to a required rate of return established by the company.

Example 3.2

A company is currently considering three potential investment projects, each with a 5-year duration, and has estimated the expected outlays and accounting profits as shown in Table 3.2.

The average accounting profit and ARRs are calculated in Table 3.3.

Table 3.2. Expected Outlays and Accounting Profits

	Year 0	Year 1	Year 2	Year 3	Year 4	Year 5
Project A	(20,000)	4,000	6,000	7,000	3,000	5,000
Project B	(20,000)	10,000	10,000	2,000	2,000	1,000
Project C	(60,000)	20,000	10,000	30,000	10,000	5,000

Table 3.3. Estimation of Accounting Rate of Return

	Average profit	Initial investment	ARR (%)
Project A	5,000	20,000	25
Project B	5,000	20,000	25
Project C	15,000	60,000	25

The strengths of ARR rest in its ease of calculation and interpretation as percentages, which is a familiar concept. In addition, unlike payback, the entire project life is considered in its calculation. However, a number of significant weaknesses are also apparent:

1. The use of both accounting profit and capital employed is somewhat problematic due to the differing accounting policies acceptable and various alternative measures for capital employed (initial capital and average capital). Consequently, several differing results could be estimated depending on the measures used.
2. As with the payback method, the time value of money is ignored, which is regarded as a major weakness. Projects A and B have comparable accounting profits over their lives, but in a significantly different pattern over time.
3. ARR is a relative rather than an absolute measure; therefore, the magnitude of the initial investment is not taken into account. Project C is a much larger project, which could prove significant when companies have limited capital to invest.

The underlying criticism of both of these traditional methods is the absence of an adjustment to take the time value of money into account. The argument is that since the expected cash flows are likely to occur over a period of several years, we cannot meaningfully compare them in their raw state and an adjustment should be made. This is achieved through the process of discounting, which converts future cash flows to a present-day equivalent value in an attempt to make comparisons more realistic.

The Discounted Cash Flow (DCF) Techniques

These techniques are characterized by the inclusion of an adjustment for the time value of money, achieved through the process of discounting. This process, the reverse of compounding, converts future cash flows to a current (present) value, which enables a comparison with the initial outlay of the project.

The process of compounding converts present values to future values using the equation

$$\text{future value} = \text{present value} \times (1 + r)^t,$$

where r is the assumed interest rate and t is the number of time periods (usually years). For example, if we invest £1,000 at an interest rate of 10% for 5 years, then the future value can be estimated using the equation

$$\text{future value} = £1,000 \times (1 + 0.1)^5 = £1,610.$$

In contrast, the process of discounting reverses the procedure by converting future values to its equivalent present value. For example, the present value of £1,000 receivable in 5 years if the interest rate is 10% per annum is given by the following:

$$\text{present value} = \text{future value}/(1 + r)^t$$

$$\text{present value} = £1,000 /(1 + 0.1)^5 = £621$$

The availability of discount tables (Appendix A) simplifies the calculation, and annuity (or cumulative present value) tables (Appendix B) are useful when the cash flows are constant each year.

Clearly, the adjustment for the time value of money increases with both time and the discount rate used (as illustrated in Table 3.4).

The discounted cash flows techniques, in contrast with the traditional techniques, use the discounting process in their evaluation of project proposals. The two main techniques in this category are net present value (NPV) and internal rate of return (IRR). The NPV method provides a solution in monetary terms, whereas IRR estimates the return as a percentage. We shall illustrate and discuss each method in turn.

Table 3.4. Discount Factors

Rate/time (%)	5 years	10 years	15 years	20 years
5	0.784	0.614	0.481	0.377
10	0.621	0.386	0.239	0.149
15	0.497	0.247	0.123	0.061
20	0.402	0.162	0.065	0.026

Net Present Value (NPV)

All forecast cash flows associated with a project are converted to present values, and the NPV is the difference between the projected discounted cash inflows and discounted cash outflows. The decision criteria are to accept projects exhibiting a positive NPV and reject projects with a negative NPV. In more formal terms, $NPV = \sum CFt/(1 + r)^t - IO$, where CFt are the cash flows at times 1, 2, 3, and so forth, and IO is the initial outlay at time 0. The use of NPV as a project evaluation technique is consistent with the objective of shareholder wealth maximization, as positive NPVs should yield an equivalent increase in shareholder wealth.

Example 3.3

The initial cost of a proposal is $20,000 and the expected cash flows for the 3-year life of the project are $10,000 in year 1, $15,000 in year 2, and $25,000 in year 3. We shall use both 15% and 20% discount rates (see Table 3.5).

From our calculations in Table 3.5, the project is acceptable at both discount rates. In addition to indicating whether the project will increase the company's value, the following are also perceived advantages of this technique:

1. Considers all the cash flows (in contrast to payback)
2. Adjusts for the time value of money (in contrast to both the traditional techniques)
3. Accounts for the risk of the project through the discount rate chosen

The following are disadvantages of NPV:

Table 3.5. NPV Estimation Using Differing Discount Rates

	15% discount factors	NPV @ 15%	20% discount factors	NPV @ 20%
(20,000)	1.000	(20,000)	1.000	(20,000)
10,000	0.870	8,700	0.833	8,330
15,000	0.756	11,340	0.694	10,410
20,000	0.658	13,160	0.579	11,580
NPV		13,200		10,320

1. It requires an estimate of the discount rate and cost of capital, which can prove problematic.
2. The NPV is expressed in monetary terms, whereas a percentage is often easier to interpret.
3. The NPV does not allow for flexibility after the project decision (see real options).
4. An inability to deal with intangible benefits decreases its usefulness for strategic projects.

Internal Rate of Return (IRR)

In simple terms, the IRR is the discount rate at which the NPV equals zero; that is, the decision maker is indifferent between accepting and rejecting the project on the basis of NPV. Rearranging our previous equation, we get $\sum CFt/(1 + r)^t - IO = 0$.

Once the IRR has been calculated, it can then be compared with the returns of other projects or investments, and a decision can be made to select the best option. The internal rate of return must be greater than or equal to a company's cost of capital in order to accept an investment. The company may require a higher rate of return, or "hurdle rate," than the cost of capital before accepting a project, particularly where higher risk is apparent.

The internal rate of return is more difficult to calculate than the NPV, as we are essentially attempting to solve a polynomial equation that invariably has multiple solutions. A common approach is to establish two rates, one generating a positive NPV and the other a negative NPV, and then to interpolate between the two.

Example 3.4

Returning to Example 3.3, we see that the project generated a positive NPV using a discount rate of 20%, which implies that the IRR of the project must be in excess of 20%. Since the NPV is quite significant at 20%, we should try a much higher discount rate when attempting to obtain a negative NPV. Consequently, we will use 50% for our higher rate and discount as shown in Table 3.6.

As we can see from our calculations, the IRR must be close to 50%, but we can use the following formula to obtain a more exact estimate:

$$IRR = Rl + \frac{NPVl}{NPVl - NPVh} \times (Rh - Rl),$$

where

- Rl and Rh are the low and high discount rates, respectively.
- NPVl and NPVh are the NPVs using the low and high rates.

If we substitute our figures into the formula, we get the following:

$$IRR = 20\% + \frac{10,320}{10,320 + 750} \times (50\% - 20\%) = 20\% + 0.932(30\%) = 48\%$$

Table 3.6. Estimation of Internal Rate of Return

	20% discount factors	NPV @ 20%	50% discount factors	NPV @ 50%
(20,000)	1.000	(20,000)	1.000	(20,000)
10,000	0.833	8,330	0.667	6,670
15,000	0.694	10,410	0.444	6,660
20,000	0.579	11,580	0.296	5,920
NPV		10,320		(750)

Therefore, the IRR of the proposed project is 48%, which comfortably exceeds the discount rate of 20% and is likely to lead to the project being accepted.

In the majority of cases, using the two DCF techniques for a project would usually give the same conclusion; that is, both accept or both reject. The IRR technique has similar advantages to NPV, in that it incorporates an adjustment for the time value of money and uses all the projected cash flows in its estimation. Moreover, the answer in percentage terms is regarded as more intuitive than the monetary values associated with NPV. However, there are two technical difficulties inherent in the calculation of IRR:

1. *The reinvestment assumption.* The method used to calculate IRR implies that the cash flows expected from the project can be reinvested at the rate calculated. In Example 3.4, we estimated an IRR of 48%, thereby assuming that the cash flows at the end of each period can be reinvested at this somewhat unrealistic rate. Even though it might be possible to invest in such a project today, there is no guarantee that similar returns will be available in each of the following periods.

2. *Multiple solutions.* This issue arises primarily as a consequence of the polynomial nature of the equation we are trying to solve for IRR. If the cash flows projected for the investment are typical, whereby an initial cash outflow is followed by a series of cash inflows, then the problem does not arise. However, where there are further cash outflows later in the project's life, the possibility of multiple solutions arises. There is a mathematical rule (Descartes' rule of signs) that suggests that the number of potential solutions is determined by the number of changes in sign. With the typical cash flow there is only one change of sign and consequently one answer. That is,

$$- \quad + \quad + \quad + \quad + \quad +$$

However, in the following case there are three changes in sign, which could yield three alternative solutions:

$$- \quad + \quad + \quad - \quad + \quad +$$

There are other occasions when NPV and IRR can result in differing recommendations. The size and duration of the project under consideration are the most common ones. Furthermore, even two projects of the same length may have different patterns of cash flow. The cash flow of one project may continuously increase over time, while the cash flow of the other project may increase, decrease, stop, or become negative.

When Are NPV and IRR Reliable?

Generally speaking, you can use and rely on both the NPV and the IRR if two conditions are met. First, if projects are compared using the NPV, a discount rate that fairly reflects the risk of each project should be chosen. There is no problem if two projects are discounted at two different rates because one project is riskier than the other. Remember that the result of the NPV is as reliable as the discount rate that is chosen. If the discount rate is unrealistic, the decision to accept or reject the project is baseless and unreliable. Second, if the IRR method is used, the project must not be accepted just because its IRR is very high. Management must ask whether such an impressive IRR is possible to maintain. In other words, management should look into past records and existing and future business to see whether an opportunity to reinvest cash flows at such a high IRR really exists. If the firm is convinced that such an IRR is realistic, the project is acceptable. Otherwise, the project must be reevaluated by the NPV method using a more realistic discount rate.

Modifications

Some of the weaknesses of the appraisal techniques discussed have been addressed by carrying out modifications to the original techniques. We shall examine alterations that have been suggested for payback and IRR.

Payback

One of the criticisms leveled at payback is its failure to account for the time value of money; therefore, discounted payback has been proposed as an improvement. The cash flows used for the payback period are discounted prior to estimating the payback period. Clearly, the effect will always be to lengthen the payback period compared to the original payback method, as shown in Example 3.5 (see Table 3.7).

Example 3.5

The undiscounted cash flows give a payback period of exactly 3 years, whereas the discounted payback lies between 3 and 4 years, or more precisely

$$\text{discounted payback} = 3 + (1{,}647/2{,}288) = 3.72 \text{ years.}$$

Although this modification addresses one of the main criticisms of payback, problems still remain with regard to measuring profitability and considering project cash flows after the payback period has been reached.

A further adjustment that addresses the problem of postpayback cash flows is the discounted payback index. The approach is to calculate the present value of the return phase of the project and divide by the present value of the investment phase. If we revisit Example 3.5, the discounted payback index (DPBI) can be calculated as

$$\text{DPBI} = 6{,}641/6{,}000 = 1.107.$$

This can be interpreted as the number of times the capital investment is covered by the subsequent project cash flows. Any value in excess of 1 indicates that the project has a positive NPV, which can be calculated as 10.7% of the initial capital investment. The index can additionally be used to estimate the time required to recover both the initial investment and the cost of finance as follows:

$$\text{recovery} = (1/\text{DPBI}) \times \text{project life} = (1/1.107) \times 4 = 3.61 \text{ years}$$

Table 3.7. Estimation of Discounted Payback Period

Year	Cash flow	Discounted at 15%	Payback	Discounted payback
0	(6,000)			
1	1,000	870	1,000	870
2	2,000	1,512	3,000	2,382
3	3,000	1,971	6,000	4,353
4	4,000	2,288		6,641

Modified IRR (MIRR)

The adjustment to IRR is more radical and involves the calculation of terminal values (TV) for each of the cash inflows using the assumption that the reinvestment rate is equal to the more conservative discount rate, as opposed to the IRR estimated.

Table 3.8 shows the results if we consider the cash flows of Example 3.3 again.

The MIRR is then obtained by estimating the rate that, when applied to the initial outlay (20,000), cumulates to 50,200 within 3 years:

$$20,000(1 + r)^3 = 50,200$$

$$\rightarrow (1 + r)^3 = 50,200/20,000 = 2.51$$

$$\rightarrow r = \sqrt[3]{2.51} - 1 = 1.359 - 1 = 0.359 \text{ or } 35.9\%$$

This result is more prudent than the 48% estimated using IRR and provides a more realistic estimate of the return on the project. However, there is some confusion about what the reinvestment rate implies. Indeed, one implication of the MIRR is that the project is not capable of generating cash flows as predicted, and that the project's NPV is overstated. The only significant advantage of the MIRR technique is that it is relatively quick to calculate and eliminates the possibility of multiple solutions.

Adjusted Present Value (APV)

The APV method permits the decision maker to separate the components of the value added by the proposed investment. Principally, it relates to the method of financing used for the project in addition to the value generated

Table 3.8. Calculation of Terminal Value

	20% FV factors	TV @ 20%
10,000	1.22	12,200
15,000	1.2	18,000
20,000	1.0	20,000
Terminal value	—	50,200

by the project itself, but can also take into account other specific costs or incentives associated with the project.

In simple terms, the APV is estimated by first calculating the "base case" NPV, which assumes the project will be financed entirely by equity. This implies that the appropriate discount rate used is derived from the company's ungeared equity beta factor.

The second stage is to value the cash flows attributable to the financing decision, which derive from any debt financing associated with the project. In essence, we are incorporating the tax shield benefit for a geared project in a similar fashion to the analysis Modigliani and Miller[1] made of geared and ungeared companies.

The NPVs obtained from these two stages are then added together to get the APV for the project. For some projects, further adjustments may be relevant to accommodate other relevant costs or benefits, such as issue costs and specific grants or subsidies.

For marginal projects, the additional NPV from the tax shield may prove decisive in determining the acceptability of the project (see Example 3.6).

Example 3.6

Sorrell Plc is considering a project that requires an initial capital outlay of £10 million, which is expected to generate annual pretax cash flows of £2.25 million in perpetuity. The project will be financed by £7 million of equity and £3 million of debt finance, on which an interest rate of 12% will be charged. The company has estimated that the required return, if the project was entirely equity financed, would be 17%. The company pays corporation tax at the rate of 30%.

Step 1: Calculate base case NPV.

$$NPV = -£10 \text{ million} + (£2.25 \text{ million} (1 - 0.30))/0.17 = -£10 \text{ million} + £9.26 \text{ million} = -£0.74 \text{ million}$$

Step 2: Calculate PV of financing.

$$PV = ((£3 \text{ million})(0.12)(0.30))/0.12 = £0.9 \text{ million}$$

Step 3: Calculate adjusted present value.

APV = –£0.74 million + £0.9 million = £0.16 million

Therefore, although the base case NPV is negative, the project is saved by the present value of the tax shield. It could be argued that the tax benefit of debt finance has distorted the investment decision for this project, which would otherwise be rejected.

Survey Evidence

The academic textbooks would suggest the following order of preference for the appraisal techniques we have discussed:

1. DCF techniques are superior to the traditional techniques, primarily on the basis of their adjustment for the time value of money, which is omitted by the traditional techniques.
2. Of the DCF techniques, NPV is superior to IRR, as it is consistent with shareholder wealth maximization and does not suffer from the theoretical problems inherent with IRR (reinvestment assumption and multiple rates of return).

Consequently, in practical application we would predict both that the NPV would be more widely used than IRR and that the DCF techniques would be more popular than the traditional methods of appraisal.

The majority of questionnaire-based studies examining corporate financial practices focus primarily on the U.S. or European markets.[2] Table 3.9 summarizes the evidence from U.S. and UK surveys.

The U.S. studies[3] find increased use of NPV as an investment appraisal technique compared to earlier empirical studies, with almost 75% of CFOs indicating that they always or almost always used these techniques. This was in marked contrast to an earlier U.S. survey,[4] in which less than 10% of large firms used NPV as a primary capital budgeting tool.

In the United Kingdom, a longitudinal study[5] conducted over the period 1975–1992 discovered an increasing incidence of DCF techniques, but payback proves to be the most popular technique over the period. With regard to the DCF techniques, it is reported that IRR is used by more companies than NPV. An additional conclusion is that the majority of companies do not rely on a single technique but instead use

Table 3.9. Survey Evidence: U.S. and UK

Technique	United States (2001)	United States (2002)	United Kingdom (1996)	United Kingdom (2000)	United Kingdom (2006)
NPV (%)	75	96	74	80	99
IRR (%)	76	95	81	81	89
Payback (%)	57	75	94	70	96
ARR (%)	20	33	50	56	60

three or even four techniques. Therefore, the techniques are seen as complementary rather than competing.

Further UK evidence[6] portrays increasing usage of, particularly, NPV and, to a lesser extent, IRR and payback. This work distinguishes between the companies surveyed on the basis of size as proxied by capital employed. Their results reveal the DCF techniques as being the most popular, with approximately 80% of companies using NPV and IRR, compared to 70% who use payback. When classified on the basis of size, it is clear that the larger companies rely more heavily on DCF techniques than their smaller counterparts, with 97% of large companies using NPV in contrast with only 62% of small companies. There is also a tendency for the smaller companies to be more prolific users of payback. Another study[7] reveals almost universal use of NPV and payback, clearly emphasizing that companies do not place reliance on a single appraisal method.

Further survey evidence, extended to a number of European countries, Australia, Japan, and Canada, is summarized in Table 3.10.

The broader European study[8] included companies from Germany, France, and the Netherlands, and overall findings suggested a lower incidence of usage across all techniques compared to U.S. and UK results. This was particularly evident for German and French companies, with payback being most popular, but only being utilized by approximately half of the companies in each country. The survey of Dutch companies revealed greater usage of all techniques, though again markedly lower than their U.S. and UK counterparts, with NPV proving the most popular technique. Again, a size effect existed, with the large companies being more likely to use the NPV approaches.

Finally, two more recent studies also provide a wider perspective, with one[9] examining capital budgeting practice in Australia and the other[10]

Table 3.10. Survey Evidence: Other Countries

Technique	Netherlands (2004)	Germany (2004)	France (2004)	Canada (2007)	Japan (2007)	Australia (2008)
NPV	70	48	35	1	3	94
IRR	56	42	44	2	1	81
Payback	65	50	51	3	2	90
ARR	25	32	16			57

including Canada, Japan, the United States, and the United Kingdom. In the second study, where rankings rather than percentage used was employed to measure popularity, IRR was the most frequently applied technique followed by NPV, but the difference is not statistically significant. Managers also continue to make extensive use of payback. A similar ranking of investment techniques is found in each country, though some variations are evident. Managers in the United Kingdom use investment appraisal techniques more often than managers in other countries, and managers in Japan use them the least. Again, a positive relation between DCF usage and firm size is obvious, which is explained by both broader practical experience and better knowledge of financial theory among managers in large companies.

The Australian evidence[11] is based on a 2004 survey of 356 firms listed on the Australian Securities Exchange and provides respondents with a choice of eight appraisal techniques (including some of the more recent innovations). The responses indicated that NPV was the most widely used technique (94%), followed by payback (91%) and IRR (80%). Most companies did not rely on a single technique, with 27% employing between one and three alternatives while the remainder regularly used more. Finally, the size effect did not appear as strong in this study, with no significant difference between small, medium, and large companies being evident.

The overall conclusions emerging from this range of empirical studies appear to conflict with the academic recommendations regarding the usage of appraisal techniques on two fronts. First, payback, despite its inherent limitations, continues to be widely used by the majority of companies; and second, IRR appears to be used as regularly as NPV, in spite of its identified theoretical difficulties.

One of the most prominent explanations for the continued use of payback is that it takes into account perceptions of risk, and that its use was positively correlated with measures of perceived uncertainty.[12] An alternative perception is that the use of payback is an adverse consequence of managerial short-termism, particularly where there is high managerial turnover, which then leads to an emphasis on early cash flows. It has also been suggested that its continued use arises from emphasizing early cash flows, about which there is more confidence; measuring the speed of return of capital; and its simplicity for the initial screening of projects.[13] Finally, it has been proposed that the maximization of NPV is more likely to occur when senior managers actively encourage the use of payback by subordinates, rather than insisting upon the use of NPV at all levels of management.[14]

Despite its much publicized theoretical difficulties, survey evidence suggests that IRR competes well with the superior NPV in its applicability to real world investment decisions. Its continuing popularity could be explained by its reporting simplicity, whereby it presents the overall return from an investment in a clear and direct manner that provides an easy decision-making process for companies to determine which investments to select. The interpretation of a percentage figure could be viewed as more intuitively appealing, particularly by managers of a nonfinancial background, than the more complex interpretation of NPV. Finally, IRR may be more convenient for the process of ranking projects.

CHAPTER 4

Cash Flows and Discount Rates

The appraisal techniques discussed in the previous chapter (with the exception of accounting rate of return) rely on establishing the expected cash flows arising from the project under consideration along with an appropriate discount (hurdle) rate to take account of the time value of money for the DCF methods.

Initially in this chapter, we shall consider the problem of identifying the relevant cash flows for inclusion in the project appraisal, together with any adjustments that may be necessary. In particular, we shall consider the potential effects of taxation and inflation on the cash flows. Subsequently, the task of estimating an appropriate discount rate (net present value [NPV]) or hurdle rate (internal rate of return [IRR]) will be addressed, which will include the estimation of an appropriate cost of capital and will also consider the impact of project risk on this decision.

Cash Flows

The costs that should be considered by a decision maker, whether facing a short- or long-term decision, are often referred to as "relevant costs," and an integral part of the decision-making process is an ability to distinguish between relevant and irrelevant costs. To be regarded as relevant, a cost should exhibit the following properties:

1. *Future*. The cost must not have already been incurred prior to the investment decision being made. Such past or "sunk" costs are irrelevant and cannot be affected by any subsequent decision. Examples of such costs would include expenditure on market research prior to considering investment in a new product or consultancy fees

incurred. Although these may not yet have been paid, they are still regarded as irrelevant, as they are a committed cost.

2. *Incremental.* This means that the cost must be caused specifically by proceeding with the project under consideration, rather than a common cost that would be incurred irrespective of whether or not the decision is made. Therefore, an allocation of corporate overheads to a project would not be regarded as relevant, since these overheads are not caused by the project itself.

3. *Cash.* With the exception of accounting rate of return (ARR), the other appraisal techniques use cash flows for valuation purposes. Consequently, costs such as depreciation or the book value of existing equipment should be excluded from the appraisal.

Opportunity Costs

Another category of costs that may be relevant for consideration is referred to as opportunity costs. An opportunity cost is defined as the benefit foregone by choosing one opportunity instead of the next best alternative. Such costs often arise as a consequence of limited resources, and involve the movement of resources from alternative uses, thereby incurring a cost elsewhere. Examples could include the following:

1. Transferring labor from a different part of the company, which may result in lost contributions
2. Introducing a new product, which may cause a decrease in revenue from existing products
3. Using a warehouse, which could be rented out for alternative use
4. Employing materials from existing stock, which could otherwise be sold

Some assumptions are made in relevant costing:

1. Cost patterns are known, that is, breakdown of fixed and variable costs and which fixed costs are attributable to a specific department or division.
2. The amounts of fixed costs, variable costs, sales demand, and sales price are known with certainty.

3. The information on which a decision is made is both complete and reliable.

Example 4.1

Henry Group Plc has spent $300,000 researching the prospects for a new range of products. If it is decided that production is to go ahead, an investment of $2,400,000 in capital equipment will be required on January 1, 2011. The accounts department has produced budgeted profit and loss statements for each of the next 5 years for the project. At the end of the fifth year, the capital equipment will be sold and production will cease. The capital equipment is expected to be sold for scrap on December 31, 2015, for $400,000 (see Table 4.1).

When production is started, it will be necessary to raise material stock levels by $400,000 and other working capital by $300,000. It may be assumed that payment for materials and other variable costs and fixed overheads are made at the end of each year. Both the additional stock and other working capital increases will be released at the end of the project. The fixed overhead figures in the budgeted accounts have two elements—60% is due to a reallocation of existing overheads, 40% is directly incurred because of the take-up of the project.

Task

Identify the relevant cash flows for each year from 2011 to 2015. The following are inclusive costs at commencement of the project:

1. The research costs fall into the category of sunk costs, as they have already been incurred and are, therefore, irrelevant to the investment decision.
2. The initial cost of the project, $2,400,000, is a relevant cost.
3. Investment in working capital (stock, debtors) is a common occurrence when considering investment in new products. The usual assumption is that the amount invested, $700,000 in this project, is a cash outflow at the beginning of the project and is liquidated in the final year of the project, resulting in a cash inflow. This amount would usually be included in the initial cost when calculating payback.

Table 4.1. Budgeted Profit and Loss Statements

	Year end Dec. 2011 (thousands of $)	Year end Dec. 2012 (thousands of $)	Year end Dec. 2013 (thousands of $)	Year end Dec. 2014 (thousands of $)	Year end Dec. 2015 (thousands of $)
Sales	5,000	5,000	5,000	4,200	3,000
Materials	3,400	3,400	3,400	2,920	2,200
Other variable costs	500	500	500	420	300
Interest costs	100	100	100	100	100
Fixed overheads	200	200	240	240	240
Depreciation	400	400	400	400	400
Net profit (loss)	400	400	360	120	(240)

The following are costs incurred during the project:

1. Interest costs should not be included if the project will be evaluated using a discounted cash flow technique, since the process of discounting takes the financing cost into account.
2. Fixed overheads should be examined carefully, and only those specifically caused by the new project should be included. Therefore, in the project in Example 4.1, only $80,000 is relevant for 2011 and 2012 and $96,000 for the remaining years, as the remainder is an allocation of existing costs.
3. Depreciation is not a cash flow, so it will always be excluded unless accounting profits are being used to evaluate the project (ARR).

The following represents cash flow at end of project:

1. The scrap value of the equipment at the end of the project, $400,000, is a relevant cost.

The revised cash flows for the project are shown in Table 4.2.

Having established the relevant cash flows for project appraisal, it may also be necessary to make additional adjustments to incorporate the impacts of taxation and inflation, which we shall now consider.

Taxation

On the assumption that the project will increase the profitability of the business, there will inevitably be a further tax liability on the increased profits. However, the magnitude of the additional tax payment may be reduced if the assets invested qualify for taxation depreciation (capital) allowances. These allowances can be used to reduce the taxable profits, and hence the tax liability arising. In addition, it is normally assumed that the additional tax is payable in the year following the liability arising, for the purpose of establishing the timing of the cash outflow.

In the United Kingdom, the allowances vary depending on the type of investment, and can take the form of either a first year allowance (FYA) or a writing-down allowance (WDA). In addition, there may be a balancing

Table 4.2. Revised Project Cash Flows

	Dec. 2011 (thousands of $)	Dec. 2012 (thousands of $)	Dec. 2013 (thousands of $)	Dec. 2014 (thousands of $)	Dec. 2015 (thousands of $)
Sales	5,000	5,000	5,000	4,200	3,000
Materials	3,400	3,400	3,400	2,920	2,200
Other variable costs	500	500	500	420	300
Fixed overheads	80	80	96	96	96
Cash flow	1,020	1,020	1,004	764	404

allowance or charge when the asset is disposed of for an amount less than or greater than its written-down value.

Example 4.2

Columbus Plc is considering the purchase of new equipment for $100,000, which will qualify for a writing-down allowance at 25% per annum. The asset is expected to have an economic life of 4 years and a residual value of $20,000.

The writing-down allowances are calculated in Table 4.3.

The allowances for each year can then be set off against the taxable profits for the profit to reduce the tax payable. At the end of the asset's economic life, the written-down value is $31,640. Therefore, a further balancing allowance of $11,640 is allowable, resulting in total capital allowances for year 4 of $22,187 ($10,547 plus $11,640). If the disposal value had been in excess of $31,640, a balancing charge would have been made, thereby reducing the allowances granted. The principle is that the total capital allowances should equal the true cost of the asset; that is, the difference between initial cost and residual value ($80,000 in the previous case).

Example 4.3

If Columbus Plc had projected the following pretax cash flows, and was subject to a tax rate of 20%, the NPV would be calculated as displayed in Table 4.4, assuming a cost of capital of 10%.

$$NPV = (100,000) + 80,000(0.909) + 89,000(0.826) + 103,750(0.751) +$$
$$68,813(0.683) - 13,563(0.621)$$

Table 4.3. Calculation of Writing-Down Allowances

Year	WDA ($)	Written-down value ($)	Balancing allowance ($)
1	25,000	75,000	—
2	18,750	56,250	—
3	14,063	42,187	—
4	10,547	31,640	11,640

Table 4.4. Pretax Cash Flows

Year	Equipment ($)	Pretax ($)	After allow ($)	Tax @ 20% ($)	Cash flow ($)
0	(100,000)				(100,000)
1		80,000	55,000		80,000
2		100,000	81,250	(11,000)	89,000
3		120,000	105,937	(16,250)	103,750
4	20,000	70,000	47,813	(21,187)	68,813
				(9,563)	(9,563)

In the current economic climate, governments are attempting to encourage companies to invest by increasing the capital allowances available. In the United States, the American Recovery and Reinvestment Act (2009) has extended through 2009 the special 50% depreciation allowance (known as bonus depreciation) and, through section 179 of the act, has also enabled small businesses to deduct up to $250,000 of the cost of qualifying assets placed in service during 2009 (without the new law this would have been only $133,000). Similarly, in the United Kingdom, the capital allowance rules for 2009–10 are that a 100% Annual Investment Allowance can be claimed up to £50,000 ($75,000), and 40% (previously 20%) capital allowance can be claimed on new asset expenditure over £50,000 ($75,000). Companies are also encouraged to invest in environmentally beneficial equipment by the availability of 100% first year allowances for such investments.

Finally, taxation can exert a less obvious influence on investment decision through its impact on the discount rate. The long-term capital structure of most companies will include a varying amount of debt financing (leverage). The interest paid to debt holders is tax deductible and, consequently, the cost of debt financing is reduced. Therefore, there is a tax incentive encouraging the use of long-term debt finance, although the increased financial risk must also be considered. The after-tax cost of debt is then input into the calculation of the weighted average cost of capital (WACC).

Inflation

Most of the major world economies currently have levels of inflation in close proximity to zero, or in some cases prices are decreasing. Furthermore, given the predictions of a relatively slow economic turnaround, it is unlikely that inflation will prove an economic problem in the near future. This would imply that inflation is somewhat irrelevant to investment decision making at this time, but investors previously encountered very real difficulties as a consequence of high inflation rates. The deep recession of the 1970s, fueled by the oil crisis, resulted in an average inflation rate of almost 14% in the United Kingdom for that decade, peaking at 25% in the summer of 1975.

When rates of inflation are significant and volatile in nature, additional problems are faced by the decision maker. Inflation increases the uncertainty already inherent in estimating future cash flows, and also influences the required rate of return by impacting the nominal cost of capital.

Inflation and Cash Flows

The existence of inflation makes the estimation of cash flows such as sales revenue, operating costs, and working capital requirements more problematic. Often, there is a tendency to assume that when revenues and costs rise proportionately, inflation will not have much impact. However, there are two weaknesses in the logic of this argument. First, it is likely that the different cash flows (revenues, material, labor costs, etc.) each show differing degrees of responsiveness to inflation. Some cash flows do not fully adjust with the general rate of inflation, while others do not adjust at all (e.g., lease payments). Second, the rate used for discounting cash flows is usually the nominal rate, and it would be both inappropriate and inconsistent to use a nominal rate to discount cash flows that are not adjusted for the effect of inflation (i.e., real cash flows).

To investigate the impact of inflation on cash flows, it is therefore important to distinguish between nominal and real cash flows. In the first case, the cash flows are expressed in terms of the purchasing value when the cash flow occurs and in the second case in terms of the purchasing value when the project is being evaluated. A common mistake is to mix real and nominal cash flows, which can occur when significant levels of inflation are predicted. In many such cases, evaluations are performed in real terms for simplicity, but there is often a failure to adjust cash flows that are contractually set (e.g., royalties).

Inflation and Rates of Return

As with cash flows, there is a choice between real and nominal rates of return. The difference between the two alternatives is a result of inflation, and an approximate relationship between the two rates is given by the equation, nominal rate – rate of inflation = real rate. For example, if the nominal interest rate is 5% and the rate of inflation is 2%, then real interest rate = 5% – 2% = 3%.

However, a more precise solution is provided by the Fisher equation, which states

$$(1 + \text{real rate})(1 + \text{inflation rate}) = (1 + \text{nominal rate}).$$

Reworking the previous example then gives

$$(1 + \text{real rate})(1.02) = 1.05.$$

Therefore,

$$\text{real rate} = (1.05/1.02) - 1 = 2.94\%.$$

The basic principle underlying the treatment of inflation is that of consistency in the use of real and nominal cash flows and discount rates. In other words, real cash flows should be discounted by real discount rates, and nominal cash flows by nominal interest rates. If real cash flows are mixed with nominal discount rates (or vice versa), there may be a tendency to erroneously reject (or accept) projects. Discounting at the nominal discount rate and failing to adjust cash flows, due in 5 years' time at a 5% anticipated annual inflation rate, will result in present values being understated by approximately 22%. The mismatch of inflation assumptions is most pronounced for longer term projects because the failure to include inflation in cash flow estimates compounds with time. Under these circumstances, distant cash flows have present values that are more seriously distorted. Such errors may explain, in part, the shift toward shorter lived projects and myopic investment decisions observed in many businesses.

Example 4.4

A project generates the money cash flows shown in Table 4.5.

A return of 15.5% is available on similar investments (nominal) and prices (Retail Price Index [RPI]) will increase by 5% per annum.

Approach 1

Discount money cash flows by the market rate of interest (Table 4.6).

Approach 2

Discount money cash flows by RPI to obtain cash flows in current purchasing power (Table 4.7).

Table 4.5. Project Money Cash Flows

Year	Cash flow ($)
0	(1,000)
1	+800
2	+600

Table 4.6. Discounted by Market Rate of Interest

Year	Cash flow ($)	Discount factors	PV ($)
0	(1,000)	1.0000	(1,000)
1	+800	0.8658	+692.64
2	+600	0.7496	+449.76
			142.40

Table 4.7. Discounted by Retail Price Index (Inflation)

Year	Cash flow ($)	Discount factors	PV ($)
0	(1,000)	1.0000	(1,000)
1	+800	0.9524	+761.92
2	+600	0.9070	+554.20

Then calculate the real discount rate and apply it to inflation adjusted cash flows (see Table 4.8).

$$\frac{(1 + 0.155)}{(1 + 0.05)} - 1 = 0.10$$

There is no truly correct method of denominating the cash flows that is both practical and feasible. The most technically correct solution is to value every cash flow in nominal terms, and compare the rate of return to a nominal rate. The downside of this approach is that it requires forecasting of every cash flow at every point in time and may only be practical in very simple scenarios. A more practical, but less accurate, solution is to use real cash flows and real rates, ensuring that the values reflect technological advances and competitive pressures and the deflating of all cash flows, which by nature are expressed in nominal terms (e.g., depreciation).

Empirical evidence investigating the practical understanding of the treatment of inflation revealed that only 53 out of the 195 responding organizations (27%) dealt with inflation correctly.[1] However, 25 respondents (13%) stated that cash flows expressed in current prices are discounted at a real discount rate. Although this approach is not theoretically correct where all cash flows do not adjust with the general rate of inflation, it may provide a reasonable approximation. Therefore, discounting current price cash flows at real discount rates may not result in significantly distorted NPV or IRR calculations. On the other hand, 85 responding organizations (44%) incorrectly used a nominal discount rate to discount current price cash flows. This would understate the reported NPV. The evidence also revealed that a further 10 respondents (5%) discounted real cash flows at a nominal discount rate (also understating NPV calculations), and 22 respondents (11%) discounted nominal cash flows at a real discount rate (thus overstating NPVs).

Table 4.8. Discounted by Real Discount Rate

Year	Cash flow ($)	Discount factors	PV ($)
0	(1,000)	1.0000	(1,000)
1	+761.92	0.9091	+692.66
2	+554.20	0.8264	+449.73
			+142.39

In summary, 49% of the respondents were understating NPVs because of the incorrect treatment of inflation in the financial appraisal. It is also likely that these respondents were understating the IRR by using current or real cash flow estimates to compute the IRR and then comparing the resulting return with a nominal discount rate. There was no significant difference between the responses of the largest and smallest organizations.

Discount Rates

The rate of return on capital investment is clearly of strategic importance. If the rate is too high, valuable opportunities can be missed; whereas if it is too low, the firm can offer only inferior returns to investors compared to its competitors. The pivotal role of the hurdle rate in the finance function should place its determination at board level within the firm. The use of discounted cash flow techniques requires the estimation of a suitable discount rate to enable the translation of expected future cash flow to its present value equivalent. NPV utilizes this rate directly in its calculation, whereas IRR uses the rate indirectly as a hurdle rate against which the IRR is compared. The two main methods of establishing a discount rate are the weighted average cost of capital (WACC) and the capital asset pricing model (CAPM).

Weighted Average Cost of Capital

The WACC represents an attempt to estimate the rate of return required to invest in the assets of the firm. However, since information regarding the market values of the assets and their required rates of return is not readily available, the WACC instead uses the market-related information for the financing sources of the firm. For this reason, WACC is only applicable when the systematic risk, including its financial component, of the assets of the firm is unaltered. Consequently, for WACC to be appropriate, any potential new projects must be similar in risk and composition to the existing assets of the firm. In addition, since the majority of companies operate in multiple lines of business, using one uniform cost of capital, such as WACC, for all assets within a company is usually incorrect. Instead, specific costs of capital should be estimated for individual divisions or projects.

The estimation of WACC is a relatively straightforward task performed by estimating the effective rate of return that the firm must pay to each category of investor (ordinary shares, preference shares, debentures), and then weighting each cost by the proportion of the total market capitalization of the firm held by each category of investor. If a firm is financed by ordinary shares and a single source of debt then the formula is $WACC = w_e r_e + w_d r_d$, where

- w_e, w_d are the weightings of equity and debt.
- r_e, r_d are the costs of equity and debt.

Alternatively, $WACC = r_e - w_d(r_e - r_d)$, since $w_e + w_d = 1$.

Example 4.5

Sorrell Plc is a quoted company financed by 300,000 ordinary shares currently trading at $10 per share, and 10,000 debenture bonds currently trading at par ($100). The cost of equity has been estimated at 12% and the cost of pretax debt at 8%. The company is subject to corporation tax at 25%.

Market Values

Equity 300,000 x £10 = $3,000,000

Debt 10,000 x £100 = $1,000,000

Cost of equity = 12%

Cost of debt = 8%(1 − 0.25) = 6%

$$WACC = \frac{\$3,000,000(12\%) + \$1,000,000(6\%)}{\$4,000,000} = 10.5\%$$

Capital Asset Pricing Model

If the business risk of the investment project differs from the current activities of the company, then the validity of WACC must be questioned. In such cases, the CAPM provides an alternative method of calculating a project-specific discount rate and will lead to improved investment decisions compared to using the WACC. Essentially, the CAPM adjusts for the risk of each specific project by estimating a project specific beta factor. The beta factor is a measure of systematic or unavoidable risk specific to the firm or project.

The first step in using the CAPM to calculate a project-specific discount rate is to obtain information on other companies with similar business activities to that of the proposed investment. More specifically, the equity beta of such companies provides a "proxy beta" on the basis that it represents the business risk of the proxy companies' business operations. An obvious difficulty that may arise is that proxy companies rarely undertake a single business activity. A possible solution is to regard the equity beta as an average of the betas of several different areas of proxy company activity, weighted by their relative shares of proxy company value. However, information regarding the relative shares of proxy company value may be difficult to obtain.

Although we may now have a proxy beta for business activity, it is likely that the proxy company also has a different financial risk. Since equity betas also reflect financial risk, a further adjustment is necessary. This is achieved by first removing the effect of financial risk from the equity beta (ungearing), and then regearing so that the proxy beta reflects the gearing and financial risk of the investing company. Again, difficulties may arise in obtaining appropriate capital structure information for ungearing equity betas. Some companies have complex capital structures with many different sources of finance, while other companies may have debt that is not traded, or may use complex sources of finance, such as convertible bonds. The simplifying assumption that the beta of debt is zero will often lead to inaccuracies in calculating the project-specific discount rate.

The proxy beta is then inserted into the CAPM equation and we get

$$E(Ri) = Rf + \beta i (E(Rm) - Rf),$$

where $E(Ri)$ is the required return on the project, Rf is the risk-free rate, βi is the proxy beta factor, and Rm is the average return on the capital market.

Example 4.6

Bramble Plc is planning to invest in a new venture that is significantly different in nature from its current operations. The company's current capital structure is composed of 70% equity and 30% debt. It has identified a company, Hedgelea Plc, which operates similar activities to the proposed new venture, and has identified the equity beta of this company as 1.0. However, Hedgelea has a different capital structure, which is composed of 60% equity and 40% debt.

Additional information available is that the risk-free rate is 4%, the equity risk premium is 6%, and both companies pay tax at 30%.

Step 1: Ungear Hedgelea's Beta

The formula for ungearing a beta factor is given by the following:

$$\beta ug = \frac{\beta g\,(Ve)}{Ve + Vd(1-t)} = \frac{1.0\,(0.6)}{0.6+0.4(0.3)} = \frac{1.0(0.6)}{(0.72)} = 0.83,$$

where

- βug, βg = ungeared and geared betas, respectively,
- Ve = value of equity,
- Vd = value of debt,
- t = tax rate.

Step 2: Regear to Take Into Account the Financial Risk of Bramble

The formula for regearing a beta factor is given by the following:

$$\beta rg = \beta ug\,(Ve + Vd(1-t))/Ve = \beta ug(1 + (1-t)Vd/Ve)$$

$$= 0.83(1 + 0.7(0.3/0.7)) = 0.83(1.3) = 1.08$$

Step 3: Use CAPM Equation to Estimate Project-Specific Discount Rate

$$E(Ri) = Rf + \beta i(E(Rm) - Rf) = 4\% + 1.08(6\%) = 10.48\%$$

It is also possible to proceed further and calculate a project-specific WACC, but this is a step that is often omitted when using the CAPM in investment appraisal.

In conclusion, theory would suggest that the CAPM is the superior method, particularly when the project under consideration differs from normal business activities. The WACC does not make any adjustment for the individual risk of projects and simply applies the same discount rates to all investments. Consequently, WACC would tend to discriminate against low-risk projects and in favor of higher risk projects by applying a discount rate that is higher or lower than that suggested by CAPM. However, CAPM is technically more difficult to apply, requiring an estimate of not only the project specific beta factor but also the risk-free rate and the return on the market portfolio. In addition, a further weakness of CAPM is that the assumption of a single-period time horizon is at odds with the multiperiod nature of investment appraisal. While CAPM variables could be assumed to remain constant in future time periods, experience would suggest that, in reality, this is not the case.

Survey Evidence

The incidence of usage of CAPM in estimating the cost of capital is summarized in Table 4.9.

A U.S. survey reported[2] that CAPM was the most popular method of estimating the cost of equity, with 73% of respondents relying mainly on the CAPM, and also cited other evidence that found that 85% of 27 best practice firms used CAPM[3]. When compared to two previous surveys of U.S. companies,[4] it also appeared that the CAPM was enjoying increased popularity.

A more recent UK study[5] also found that the CAPM was the most popular method of estimating the cost of capital, but only 47% of companies surveyed used the method. A European survey[6] found a similar lower level of CAPM usage, with rates ranging from 34% to 56% across four countries. Finally, a study comparing investment practices in the United States and Canada reported that WACC was more popular in the United States than in Canada.[7]

Other evidence presented[8] suggested that the majority of respondents reviewed the cost of capital on an annual basis (54%), with a further 18%

Table 4.9. Empirical Evidence of CAPM Usage

	United States (1998)	United States (2001)	United Kingdom (2004)	Netherlands (2004)	Germany (2004)	France (2004)
Usage (%)	85	73	47	56	34	45

reviewing on a quarterly basis. More detailed narrative responses specifically mentioned that reviews occurred when interest rates changed and when major projects were under consideration.

A related, but comparatively unexplored, field of research has investigated the role of hurdle rates in the analysis of investment decisions. More specifically, the existence of differences between the hurdle rates applied and the cost of capital (discount rate) has been investigated in attempting to explain underinvestment or overinvestment. Relatively few direct studies of hurdle rates have been reported, perhaps as a consequence of hurdle rates being unrecorded and surveys of managers being the only viable method of research. Consequently, it is difficult to obtain consistent observation over time. The main evidence surveyed CEOs at Fortune 1000 companies regarding their hurdle rates. Considerable variation across the sample was reported, but the authors were unable to explain the variation despite incorporating a large number of financial and structural variables into the study. However, it was evident that the hurdle rates applied were "distinctly higher than equity holders' average rates of return and much higher than the return on debt."[9] A smaller study[10] covering 12 large manufacturing firms found hurdle rates around 15%, with some companies as high as 60%. In both these studies, the use of hurdle rates in considerable excess of the cost of capital appeared prevalent.

Very recently, research analyzed a sample of business units from the Profit Impact of Marketing Strategy database and reported almost equal numbers of business units using hurdle rates above and below the discount rate.[11] The analysis identified three sets of influences in affecting whether the hurdle rate will be above or below the discount rate. These three influences were the opportunity for discretionary behavior, the motivation or incentive to behave in a strategic fashion, and the risk in the business environment.

CHAPTER 5

Risk and Uncertainty

A typical capital investment project evaluation requires many input variables including, inter alia, sales revenues, operating expenditure, project life, interest rates, and residual values. Some of these variables may be estimated with a relatively high degree of confidence, whereas others may exhibit high levels of uncertainty. The degree of uncertainty is also likely to be a function of both the type of project and the industry within which the firm operates. For example, investments of a strategic nature are generally more problematic for industry sectors such as oil and gas.

Large, capital-intensive projects in the oil and gas industries require substantial—and mostly risky—investments in the acquisition, exploration, and subsequent operation and maintenance of new organizational assets. The decision of whether or not to invest in a new capital project commences with critical decisions during the exploration phase of a new development or expansion of an existing field. The decision-making tools used to analyze project risk will help companies to determine the probability of success or loss, and will drive the decision whether to develop or abandon the well. Of paramount importance is the development of detailed cash flow analyses to determine, as accurately as possible, the expected returns under the varying conditions of uncertainty during the expected productive life of the project.

The basic definition of risk is that the final outcome of a decision, such as an investment, may differ from that which was expected when the decision was made. We tend to distinguish between risk and uncertainty in terms of the availability of probabilities; that is, risk is when the probabilities of the possible outcomes are known (tossing a coin, spinning a die), whereas uncertainty is where the randomness cannot be expressed in terms of specific probabilities. However, it has been suggested that in the real world, it is generally not possible to allocate probabilities to potential outcomes and, therefore, the concept of risk is largely redundant.

Probability

The term probability refers to the likelihood, or chance, that a certain event will occur and takes on values ranging from zero (the event will not occur) to one (the event will definitely occur). For example, the probability of tails occurring when tossing a coin is 0.5 and the probability of a die showing the value 4 is 0.166 (1/6). The total of all the probabilities from all the possible outcomes must equal 1; that is, some outcome must occur. A real world example could be that of a company forecasting potential future sales from the introduction of a new product in year 1 (see Table 5.1).

From Table 5.1, it is clear that the most likely outcome is sales of $1,000,000, as that value has the highest probability.

Independent and Conditional Events

An independent event occurs when the outcome does not depend on the outcome of a previous event. For example, assuming that a die is unbiased, the probability of throwing a five on the second throw does not depend on the outcome of the first throw.

In contrast, with a conditional event, the outcomes of two or more events are related; that is, the outcome of the second event depends on the outcome of the first event. For example, in Table 5.1, the company is forecasting sales for the first year of the new product. If the company attempted to predict the sales revenue for the second year, it is likely that the predictions made will depend on the outcome for year 1. If the outcome for year 1 was sales of $1,500,000, the predictions for year 2 are likely to be more optimistic than if the sales in year 1 were $500,000.

The availability of information regarding the probabilities of the potential outcomes allows the calculation of both an expected value for the outcome and a measure of variability, or dispersion, of the potential

Table 5.1. Forecasted Future Sales and Expected Probabilities

Sales ($)	500,000	700,000	1,000,000	1,250,000	1,500,000
Probability	0.1	0.2	0.4	0.2	0.1

outcomes around the expected value (most typically standard deviation). The latter measure provides us with a measure of risk that can be used to assess the likely outcome.

Expected Values and Dispersion

Having the information regarding the potential outcomes and their associated probabilities, the expected value of the outcome is calculated simply by multiplying the values associated with the potential outcome by their probabilities. Referring back to Table 5.1 regarding the sales forecast, the expected value of the sales for year 1 is given by the following:

$$\text{Expected value} = (\$500{,}000)(0.1) + (\$700{,}000)(0.2) + (\$1{,}000{,}000)(0.4) + (\$1{,}250{,}000)(0.2) + (\$1{,}500{,}000)(0.1)$$

$$= \$50{,}000 + \$140{,}000 + \$400{,}000 + \$250{,}000 + \$150{,}000$$

$$= \$990{,}000$$

In this example, the expected value is very close to the most likely outcome, but this not always the case. Moreover, it is likely that the expected value does not correspond to any of the individual potential outcomes. For example, the average score from throwing a die is $(1 + 2 + 3 + 4 + 5 + 6)/6 = 3.5$, and the average family supposedly has 2.4 children. A further point regarding the use of expected values is that the probabilities are based on the event occurring repeatedly, whereas, in reality, most events only occur once.

In addition to expected value, it is also informative to have an idea of the risk or dispersion of the potential actual outcomes around the expected value. The most common measure of dispersion is the standard deviation, which is the square root of the variance and can be illustrated by an example concerning the potential returns from two investments (see Table 5.2).

To estimate the standard deviation we must first calculate the expected values of each investment:

Investment A:

$$\text{expected value} = (8\%)(0.25) + (10\%)(0.5) + (12\%)(0.25) = 10\%$$

Table 5.2. Investment Returns and Associated Probabilities

Investment A		Investment B	
Returns (%)	Probability of return	Returns (%)	Probability of return
8	0.25	5	0.25
10	0.5	10	0.5
12	0.25	15	0.25

Investment B:

$$\text{expected value} = (5\%)(0.25) + (10\%)(0.5) + (15\%)(0.25) = 10\%$$

The calculation of standard deviation proceeds by subtracting the expected value from each of the potential outcomes, followed by squaring the result and multiplying by the probability. The results are then totaled to yield the variance, and, finally, the square root is taken to give the standard deviation shown in tables 5.3 and 5.4.

In this example, although investments A and B have the same expected return, investment B is more risky because it exhibits a higher standard deviation. More commonly, the expected return and standard deviations from investments and projects are both different, but can still be compared by using the coefficient of variation, which combines the expected return and standard deviation into a single figure.

Table 5.3. Investment A

Returns (%)	Expected return (%)	Returns minus expected returns (%)	Squared (%)	Probability	Column 4 × column 5 (%)
8	10	−2	4	0.25	1
10	10	0	0	0.5	0
12	10	2	4	0.25	1
				Variance	2
				Standard deviation	1.414

Table 5.4. Investment B

Returns (%)	Expected return (%)	Returns minus expected returns (%)	Squared (%)	Probability	Column 4 × column 5 (%)
5	10	–5	25	0.25	6.25
10	10	0		0.5	0
15	10	5	25	0.25	6.25
				Variance	12.5
				Standard deviation	3.536

Coefficient of Variation and Standard Error

The coefficient of variation is calculated by dividing the standard deviation by the expected return (or mean). That is,

coefficient of variation = standard deviation/expected return.

Assume that investment X has an expected return of 20% and a standard deviation of 15%, whereas investment Y has an expected return of 25% and a standard deviation of 20%. The coefficients of variation for the two investments will be the following:

Investment X = 15%/20% = 0.75

Investment Y = 20%/25% = 0.80

The interpretation of these results would be that investment X is less risky on the basis of a lower coefficient of variation.

A final statistic relating to dispersion is the standard error, which is a measure often confused with the standard deviation. The standard deviation is a measure of the variability of a sample, which is used as an estimate of the variability of the population from which the sample was drawn. When we calculate the sample mean, we are usually interested not in the mean of this particular sample, but in the mean of the population from which the sample comes. The sample mean will vary from sample to sample; the way this variation occurs is described by the "sampling distribution" of the mean. We can also estimate how much sample means will vary from the standard deviation of this sampling distribution, which we call the standard error (SE) of the estimate of the mean. The standard error of the sample mean depends on both the standard deviation and the sample size:

$$SE = SD/ \sqrt{(\text{sample size})}.$$

The standard error falls as the sample size increases, as the extent of chance variation is reduced. However, the increase in sample size necessary to reduce the standard error by 50% is a fourfold increase due to the square root of the sample size being utilized. By contrast, the standard deviation will not tend to change as we increase the size of our sample.

Adjusting for Risk

The available techniques range from the relatively simple (risk-adjusted discount rates, certainty equivalents, reduced payback periods) to the application of probabilities (expected values) to the more complex techniques (sensitivity analysis and simulation). We shall assess the strengths and weaknesses of each of the methods and summarize available survey evidence in relating theory to practice.

Risk-Adjusted Discount Rates

The concept is simple in that the discount rate used reflects the perceived risk of the specific project under consideration. Clearly, more risky projects should be subjected to higher discount rates and lower risk projects to lower rates. The main questions to be addressed when using this technique are the following:

1. How much of a risk premium should be added for riskier projects?
2. Can we easily classify prospective projects into risk categories?

Example 5.1

Glenfield Plc has decided to use risk-adjusted discount rates for assessing new projects and has established the following discount rates for each category of project:

- Risk-free rate: 5%
- Low-risk projects: 8%
- Medium-risk projects: 12%
- High-risk projects: 20%

The approach is easy to use but is criticized for being somewhat arbitrary in nature. Furthermore, an equal adjustment to the discount rate over all periods does not reflect differences in the degree of uncertainty across periods. If the projected cash flows across periods have different degrees of uncertainty, the risk adjustment of the cash flows should also vary accordingly.

Certainty Equivalent (CE)

Risk-adjusted discount rates make an adjustment to the denominator of the equation, whereas the certainty equivalent approach adjusts the numerator (i.e., the cash flows). The CE method is derived from utility theory and relies on the decision maker being able to evaluate the risk of a cash flow and then specify an amount, to be received with certainty, that would make him or her indifferent between receiving the two cash flows. In general, people are risk averse and the lower the certainty equivalent is, the greater the degree of risk aversion. Once the certainty equivalent cash flows have been estimated, the NPV of the project is obtained by discounting at the risk-free rate.

Example 5.2

The finance director of Arnold Plc is considering the use of certainty equivalents as a mechanism of adjusting for the riskiness of project cash flows. He has decided to apply a certainty equivalent coefficient of 0.7 to risky cash flows for the project in Table 5.5 prior to calculating the NPV using a risk-free rate of 6%.

The certainty equivalent method is simple and can easily accommodate differential risk among cash flows by utilizing differing certainty equivalent coefficients. In the previous example, we could apply, for instance, 0.7, 0.6, and 0.5, respectively, to allow for increasing uncertainty. However, there is no practical method of estimating certainty

Table 5.5. *Use of Certainty Equivalents*

Year	Projected cash flows	Certainty equivalents	Present value @ 6%
0	(10,000)	(10,000)	(10,000)
1	4,000	2,800	2,640
2	8,000	5,600	4,984
3	5,000	3,500	2,940
			NPV = +$564

equivalents, and estimates could vary significantly between individuals. A further complication is that the certainty equivalents should reflect the risk preferences of the shareholders rather than the management. For these reasons, the popularity of certainty equivalents is relatively low in corporate decision making.

Reduced Payback

Perhaps the simplest adjustment to allow for the effects of uncertainty is to reduce the required payback period for the project. Since payback emphasizes the importance of cash flows in the early years of the project's life, its reduction concentrates even more on these cash flows, which are deemed to be the most certain of the projected cash flows. Therefore, by reducing the required payback period, we allow for risk by reducing the project's dependence on later cash flows. The magnitude of the reduction applied, compared to the normal payback criterion employed by the firm, would logically relate to the riskiness of the project. However, a degree of subjectivity is inherent in the process as a consequence of the decision makers' perceptions of the risk involved in the project coupled with their own degree of risk aversion.

A recent survey by AT&T[1] questioned U.S. and European CIOs and other top IT executives in multinational companies concerning the impact of the current recession on their investment in IT. The following sample is indicative of the responses regarding the shortened horizon for evaluating IT projects:

Our time period has narrowed by about 50%, roughly from two to three years, to 12–18 months. This has forced us to focus on projects that give at least 100% ROI in 12 months. Others get dropped.

ROI time frame has been narrowed from three years to one year. This has resulted in a shift to cost containment and quicker payback projects.

Using Probability in Project Appraisal

Earlier in this chapter, we introduced the concepts of expected values and standard deviation as measures of return and risk. The same methodology can be applied to the calculation of an expected NPV (ENPV) and the risk as measured by the standard deviation of the NPV.

Example 5.3

YK Oil is considering drilling two wells in close proximity to each other. It will drill one well immediately and the other in 1 year. However, it must hire the necessary equipment for both wells immediately, at a cost of $1,500,000. Geophysicists employed by the company have estimated that the first well will generate three possible revenues with associated probabilities (see Table 5.6).

The outcomes for the second well will be influenced by the outcomes from the first well as shown in Table 5.7.

The company applies a discount rate of 20% to new exploration projects, which results in the nine possible outcomes displayed in Table 5.8, with joint probabilities calculated by combining the probabilities for each well. Therefore,

$$\text{ENPV} = \$1,560,710 - \$1,500,000 = \$60,710.$$

The risk associated with the project can be measured by calculating the standard deviation of the project as shown in Table 5.9.

$$\text{standard deviation of project} = \sqrt{3.85661\text{E}+11} = \$621,016$$

Table 5.6. Well 1

Revenue ($)	Probability
$500,000	0.3
$1,000,000	0.5
$2,000,000	0.2

Table 5.7. Outcomes for Well 2 Dependent on Well 1

Well 1 ($)	Well 2 ($)	Probability
$500,000	$500,000	0.6
	$1,000,000	0.3
	$2,000,000	0.1
$1,000,000	$500,000	0.2
	$1,000,000	0.7
	$2,000,000	0.1
$2,000,000	$500,000	0.1
	$1,000,000	0.6
	$2,000,000	0.3

Table 5.8. Calculation of Expected Present Value

Outcome	NPV	Joint probabilities	EPV
1	763,500	0.18	137,430
2	1,110,500	0.09	99,945
3	1,804,500	0.03	54,135
4	1,180,000	0.10	118,000
5	1,527,000	0.35	534,450
6	2,221,000	0.05	110,050
7	2,013,000	0.02	40,260
8	2,360,000	0.12	283,200
9	3,054,000	0.06	183,240
			1,560,710

Table 5.9. Standard deviation of project.

Outcome	NPV – ENPV	(NPV – ENPV)²	Prob × (NPV-ENPV)²
1	(797,200)	$(797,200)^2$	$(797,200)^2 \times 0.18$
2	(450,210)	$(450,210)^2$	$(450,210)^2 \times 0.09$
3	243,790	$243,790^2$	$243,790^2 \times 0.03$
4	(380,710)	$(380,710)^2$	$(380,710)^2 \times 0.10$
5	(33,710)	$(33,710)^2$	$(33,710)^2 \times 0.35$
6	660,290	$660,290^2$	$660,290^2 \times 0.05$
7	452,290	$452,290^2$	$452,290^2 \times 0.02$
8	799,290	$799,290^2$	$799,290^2 \times 0.12$
9	1,493,290	$1,493,290^2$	$1,493,290^2 \times 0.06$
Variance = 3.85661E+11			

Sensitivity Analysis

Sensitivity analysis is used to investigate how "sensitive" the value of an investment project is to changes in the input variables. If a small change in the value of a variable results in a relatively large change in the outcome, then the project is said to be sensitive to that variable. The typical project may involve a significant number of input variables, but only a small number of these variables may be crucial in determining the acceptability of the project. Therefore, one of the objectives of sensitivity analysis is to identify the most significant variables so that further time and effort can be devoted to ascertaining their accuracy when evaluating the project.

In a typical investment project, input variables include the following:

- Initial cost
- Selling price
- Variable costs (materials, labor)
- Sales volume
- Residual value
- Discount rate
- Project life

An initial sensitivity analysis could be performed by simply changing each of the variables by 5% or 10% and examining the impact of the change on the original NPV, which was calculated on the basis of initial estimated values of the variables.

Example 5.4

Ryan Plc wishes to perform a sensitivity analysis on the following variables estimated for a potential investment project introducing a new product. The initial estimates for the values of the variable are shown in Table 5.10.

$$NPV = 25,000(0.8)(2.487) + 10,000(0.751) - 50,000 = \$7,250$$

We can examine the effect of an adverse 10% change in each of the variables on the estimated NPV in Table 5.11.

Table 5.10. Base Figures and NPV

Variable	
Initial cost	$50,000
Selling price per unit	$2
Variable cost per unit	$1.20
Sales volume	25,000 units
Residual value	$10,000
Discount rate	10%
Project life	3 years

Table 5.11. Impact of 10% Change in Base Values

Variable	10% change	NPV	% change in NPV
Initial cost	$55,000	$2,250	−69%
Selling price per unit	$1.80	($5,185)	−171.5%
Variable cost per unit	$1.32	($211)	−103%
Sales volume	22,500	$2,276	−69%
Residual value	$9,000	$6,499	−10%
Discount rate	11%	$6,190	−15%

From these results we can conclude that the project is particularly sensitive to changes in the selling price and variable cost. On the other hand, the NPV is relatively insensitive to changes in the residual value and discount rate. The company should therefore focus attention on the assumptions regarding selling price and variable cost to ensure the estimates are realistic.

More typically, sensitivity analysis calculates the percentage change in each of the variables that would result in an NPV equal to zero (i.e., the project is just acceptable). That is,

$$NPV = Vol(contribution)(annuity\ factor) + residual(discount\ factor) - initial\ costs = zero.$$

Initial Cost

This is perhaps the simplest variable to consider as any increase in initial cost is matched by a similar decrease in NPV. Therefore, the required change in initial cost is simply $7,250 (i.e., the initial value of the NPV).

Selling Price and Variable Cost

We shall consider these two variables together as they both impact contribution per unit. If we initially calculate the contribution per unit, which equates to an NPV equal to zero, then selling price and variable cost can easily be obtained.

$$25,000(contribution)(2.487) + 10,000(0.751) - 50,000 = 0$$

$$62,175(contribution) = 42,490 \rightarrow contribution = \$0.68\ per\ unit$$

Therefore, either the selling price per unit can decrease by $0.12 or the variable cost can increase by $0.12.

Sales Volume

$$Volume(0.80)(2.487) + 10,000(0.751) - 50,000 = 0$$

$$1.99 \times volume = 42,490 \rightarrow volume = 21,350\ Units$$

Residual Value

The treatment of residual value is similar to initial cost, except that the residual value occurs in 3 years' time, so the reduction in residual value when discounted must equal $7,250. That is,

$$\text{Reduction in residual} \times 0.751 = \$7,250 \rightarrow \text{Reduction} = \$9,654$$

Discount Rate

By definition, the internal rate of return (IRR) is the discount rate that provides an NPV equal to zero; therefore, we perform an IRR calculation.

Previously, a 10% discount rate gave a positive NPV equal to $7,250; therefore, the IRR must be higher than 10%. We could try 20%:

$$\text{NPV} = 25,000(0.8)(2.107) + 10,000(0.579) - 50,000 = -\$2,070.$$

Interpolating,

$$\text{IRR} = 10\% + (7250/9320)(10\%) = 17.8\%.$$

The changes in the variables are summarized in Table 5.12.

Our previous results are again confirmed, with the acceptability of the project particularly sensitive to changes in selling price (6%) and variable cost (10%) and relatively insensitive to changes in residual value (96.5%) and discount rate (78%).

One of the obvious drawbacks of sensitivity analysis is that we are examining the effect of changes in each variable in isolation. In reality, it may be more realistic to examine the potential impact of multiple variables changing simultaneously. In addition, sensitivity analysis does not address the probability of changes in the variables occurring.

Table 5.12. Summary of Variable Sensitivities

Variable	Absolute change	Change (%)
Initial cost	$7,250	14.5
Selling price per unit	$0.12	6.0
Variable cost per unit	$0.12	10.0
Sales volume	3,650 units	14.6
Residual value	$9,654	96.5
Discount rate	7.8%	78.0

Scenario Analysis

This technique overcomes one of the limitations of sensitivity analysis by examining potential changes in all the variables simultaneously. This is achieved by estimating a best-case and worst-case scenario for each variable and then for the project as a whole (see Table 5.13).

We then proceed to calculate the NPV under each of the two scenarios as follows:

NPV(Worst) = 20,000(0.45)(2.402) + 8,000(0.712) − 53,000 = −$25,686

NPV(Best) = 27,500(1)(2.531) + 10,000(0.772) − 48,000 = +$29,323

The decision regarding the project would then depend on the attitude toward risk. Although the NPV of the best outcome may appear attractive, the firm may not be willing to subject itself to the risk of losing $25,686, even though this outcome only results from the worst value occurring for all variables.

Scenario analysis, therefore, provides a range of potential outcomes for the project, although, again, as with sensitivity analysis, probability is not incorporated into the analysis. Therefore, the likelihood of the best-case or worst-case scenarios occurring is not apparent.

Table 5.13. Potential Scenario Values

Variable	Current value	Worst case	Best case
Initial cost ($)	50,000	53,000	48,000
Selling price per unit ($)	2	1.75	2.10
Variable cost per unit ($)	1.20	1.30	1.10
Sales volume (units)	25,000	20,000	27,500
Residual value ($)	10,000	8,000	11,000
Discount rate (%)	10	12	9

Simulation

In contrast to sensitivity and scenario analysis, simulation (or Monte Carlo simulation) more explicitly incorporates risk into project evaluation by including probabilities when considering the input variables. The construction and operation of a risk simulation model for an investment appraisal application involves a number of steps:

1. Build an investment appraisal model using discounted cash flow.
2. For each year's net cash flow, create a probability distribution and link it to a random number generator. A random number function is available in Excel (RAND or RANDBETWEEN) or random number tables could be used.
3. Carry out a simulation by drawing a value from each probability distribution using the random number generator, and sum the resulting estimates to provide an overall estimate for project NPV.
4. Repeat the simulation many times (i.e., 500 or more) to provide an estimated distribution of NPV for the project.
5. Decide whether the probability that the project NPV may be negative is, or is not, an acceptable risk and proceed accordingly.

Example 5.5

Glencree Plc is evaluating a potential investment project that costs $20,000 and is expected to have a useful economic life of 3 years. The finance director has predicted the cash flows and associated probabilities for each year as displayed in Table 5.14.

1. The discount rate applied by the company is 10% per annum.
2. Random numbers are attached to each of the possible cash flows in accordance with the estimated probabilities (see Table 5.15).

Table 5.14. Cash Flows With Probabilities

Year	Cash flow	Probability
1	$8,000	0.4
2	$10,000	0.4
3	$15,000	0.2

Table 5.15. Allocation of Random Numbers

Cash flow	Probability	Random numbers
$8,000	0.4	00–39
$10,000	0.4	40–79
$15,000	0.2	80–99

3. Generate random numbers sufficient for five simulations (i.e., 15 random numbers), as shown in Table 5.16.
4. Use random numbers to allocate cash flows as displayed in Table 5.17.
5. Calculate NPVs using discount rate of 10% (see Table 5.18).

From these results, we could generate an expected NPV by averaging the five results, which gives +4,562 and a standard deviation of 5,011. In practice, we would repeat the exercise to give perhaps 500 simulations of the cash flows and make a decision on the basis of the results generated.

Table 5.16. Generation of Random Numbers for Runs

Simulation 1	Simulation 2	Simulation 3	Simulation 4	Simulation 5
54	67	32	99	13
27	41	53	40	76
4	71	9	80	30

Table 5.17. Cash Flow Generation Using Random Numbers

Simulation 1 ($)	Simulation 2 ($)	Simulation 3 ($)	Simulation 4 ($)	Simulation 5 ($)
10,000	10,000	8,000	15,000	8,000
8,000	10,000	10,000	10,000	10,000
8,000	10,000	8,000	15,000	8,000

Table 5.18. Estimation of NPV for Runs

Year	Simulation 1 ($)	Simulation 2 ($)	Simulation 3 ($)	Simulation 4 ($)	Simulation 5 ($)
0	(20,000)	(20,000)	(20,000)	(20,000)	(20,000)
1	9,091	9,091	7,272	13,635	7,272
2	6,608	8,260	8,260	8,260	8,260
3	6,008	7,510	6,008	11,265	6,008
NPV	+1,707	+4,861	+1,540	+13,160	+1,540

Portfolio Theory

Typically, with project evaluation we consider each project in isolation. However, the overall risk of the firm's investments will depend to a large extent on the degree to which the returns on individual projects are related to each other. Portfolio theory suggests that risk can be reduced through the process of diversifying into different areas of operation. Indeed, the risk benefits are greater when the returns from the investments have little association.

Portfolio theory uses the familiar concepts of the mean return and the variance of returns (or standard deviation of returns) to measure return and risk, respectively. However, of greater significance is the degree of association between the returns on the projects as measured by the coefficient of correlation (generally denoted by r). This coefficient is limited to values between -1 and $+1$, where -1 is interpreted as perfect negative correlation, a value of zero denotes no correlation and $+1$ is perfect positive correlation.

For the purpose of reducing risk, the optimum value of the correlation coefficient is -1, with little benefit obtained from high positive correlation. The risk (as measured by standard deviation) of a portfolio consisting of two investments can be calculated as

$$Risk_{12} = \sqrt{w1^2\sigma1^2 + w2^2\sigma2^2 + 2w1w2\sigma1\sigma2\rho12},$$

where

- $w1$ and $w2$ are the weights of the two investments,
- $\sigma1$ and $\sigma2$ are the standard deviations of the two investments,
- $\rho12$ is the correlation coefficient between the returns of the two investments.

Example 5.6

Options Plc is currently considering investing in two investment projects and has estimated the mean return and standard deviation of the projects as displayed in Table 5.19.

Table 5.19. Return and Risk of Projects

Project	Mean return (%)	Standard deviation (%)
AB	10	18
XY	15	28

The company is unsure of the correlation coefficient between the two projects and is examining the effect of varying the coefficient as follows:

1. +0.5
2. 0
3. –0.5

Available funds will be invested in the two projects, with 60% invested in AB and 40% in XY.

By calculating the risk under each of the correlation coefficients, we get the following:

$$\text{Risk using} + 0.5 = \sqrt{(0.6)^2(18)^2 + (0.4)^2(28)^2 + 2(0.6)(0.4)(18)(28)(0.5)}$$
$$= 19.05\%$$

$$\text{Risk using } 0 = \sqrt{(0.6)^2(18)^2 + (0.4)^2(28)^2}$$
$$= 15.59\%$$

$$\text{Risk using} -0.5 = \sqrt{(0.6)^2(18)^2 + (0.4)^2(28)^2 - 2(0.6)(0.4)(18)(28)(0.5)}$$
$$= 11\%$$

Survey Evidence

The overall perception from published surveys is that of a general increase in the extent of risk analysis in project appraisal over time, perhaps partly a reaction to an increasingly uncertain economic environment and the availability of computer software. This is perhaps best represented on a longitudinal basis by comparing the UK evidence as summarized in Table 5.20.

In the United States, a survey of U.S. senior financial officers suggested that the challenge of dealing with risk and uncertainty was one of the most prominent problems faced by decision makers in capital budgeting.[2] Also in the United States, other evidence reported a significant

Table 5.20. Empirical Evidence of Usage of Risk Analysis Techniques

Techniques	1996 (%)	2000 (%)	2006 (%)
Sensitivity analysis	86	85	89
Reduced payback	59	20	75
Risk-adjusted rate	64	52	82
Probability analysis	47	31	77
Beta analysis	20	3	43

increase in the use of at least one formal method of risk assessment or adjustment, from 39% of responding firms in 1975 to 59% in 1980.[3] In the United Kingdom an even more dramatic increase was reported, increasing from 26% of firms in 1975 to 86% of the same firms in 1986.[4] Despite such increases, it was apparent at that time that generally the simpler techniques predominated (risk adjusted discount rates, reduced payback) as opposed to the more complex probability based techniques (sensitivity analysis, probability analysis, simulation). It was suggested that the use of more sophisticated techniques made the proposals more difficult to accept and reduced managers' enthusiasm to generate ideas. Moreover, there was no underlying evidence that the use of probabilistic techniques either caused a significant change in capital expenditure or improved corporate profitability.

Indeed, a survey of the largest 350 companies in the United Kingdom[5] reported that 68% of the respondents regularly made a subjective or intuitive evaluation of the risk involved. Of the formal risk measurement techniques, sensitivity analysis predominated, being used by 85% of companies, while 51% reported use of basic probability analysis. They also suggested that a difference existed between UK managers, who generally adjusted the discount rate for risk, and U.S. managers, who instead tended to adjust the cash flow for risk. Finally, though management tended to focus on each project individually (79%), a majority (60%) also considered the effect of project risk on the overall corporate risk-return relationship.

Most recently, two UK surveys[6] reporting evidence in 2000 and 2006 revealed comparable results for sensitivity analysis (85% and 89%, respectively), but significant differences between the other techniques.

The later study reported much higher usage of probability analysis (71%) and reduced payback (75%), though their focus was primarily on strategic investment projects, which may go some way to explaining the differences. The latter study also reported significant use of beta analysis, in contrast to earlier surveys.

CHAPTER 6

Capital Rationing

Previously, it was implicitly assumed that if a project received a positive evaluation, funds would be available for the investment to proceed. However, capital rationing refers to the situation in which capital (finance) is limited to the extent that it is not feasible to invest in all projects deemed acceptable. In such circumstances, the decision maker is faced with allocating a limited amount of capital, thereby necessitating a choice between competing projects. The assumption is generally made that the capital constraint is a short-term phenomenon (one period), perhaps arising as a consequence of the time required to raise external finance.

The capital constraint may be imposed internally by managerial decisions (soft capital rationing) or originate from the capital markets (hard capital rationing).

Soft Capital Rationing

This is a self-imposed limit placed on the capital available for investment projects. Although the objective of shareholder wealth maximization would suggest that all positive NPV projects should be accepted, there may be valid reasons why firms may wish to limit investment. These may include the following:

1. Divisional managers may habitually overstate their financing requirements for capex projects on the basis that they will not get what they request. A lot of senior management time and effort may then be unnecessarily expended on negotiating and deciding appropriate allocations of investment funds. A simpler solution is to impose a limit on funds available, and give divisional management discretion over the spending of those funds.

2. The firm may be reluctant to access the capital markets and raise additional finance for various reasons, which may include, inter alia, the cost involved and avoiding the dilution of equity, which may, in turn, impinge on earnings per share.

3. Smaller companies may wish to control the growth in their activities to reduce the dangers of overtrading. Although growth is generally desirable, uncontrolled growth can lead to excessive requirements for working capital, which may threaten those companies with a relatively small capital base.

4. A high degree of risk aversion among senior management may manifest itself in capital rationing designed to deter the acceptance of low NPV projects that may have significant downside risk.

5. There may also be nonfinancial factors contributing to the decision to limit capital, such as a shortage of a suitably skilled staff that has the ability to successfully implement projects.

The impact of soft capital rationing can be reduced or even eliminated by a managerial decision to release finance for additional funds. In theory, this can be done at any time and should not prevent the firm taking advantage of attractive investment opportunities when the need for finance arises.

Hard Capital Rationing

In contrast to soft capital rationing, which is internally imposed, hard capital rationing is externally imposed on the firm by the capital markets. More specifically, the firm is unable to borrow additional debt finance, perhaps due to a precarious financial position (i.e., impending bankruptcy) or as a consequence of a debt covenant that prevents further funds being borrowed. In reality, hard capital rationing is probably of little significance as far as investment decisions in companies are concerned. However, if it did exist, NPV analysis becomes almost impossible due to an inability to establish a cost of capital.

Assumptions

When considering capital rationing problems, we generally assume the following:

1. Each project can only be undertaken once; that is, we cannot simply identify the best project and repeat it until the capital constraint is reached.
2. Projects are divisible so that fractional investment in projects is possible, with the same proportion of NPV being received.

Solving the Problem

Air Kraft Ltd. has identified seven investment projects yielding positive NPV as shown in Table 6.1. The total investment required to invest in all the projects would be $280,000, but the firm has decided to limit capital expenditure in this period to $200,000. Each project is divisible but not repeatable.

We might initially approach the problem by choosing the project with the highest NPV and continuing on in this manner until the budget has been reached, as shown in Table 6.2.

Since the company has decided to limit spending to $200,000, we could invest in projects P, Q, U, and R to the amounts required but would only have sufficient funds to invest $40,000 in project S, which equates to 0.66 or 66.6% of the project and would yield 66.6% of the NPV of project S ($5,100 × 0.66 = $3,400). In total, from this combination of projects, we would obtain an NPV of $31,900.

Table 6.1. Potential Projects Identified

Project	Initial cash outlay ($)	NPV ($)
P	($20,000)	$8,000
Q	($70,000)	$7,200
R	($40,000)	$6,500
S	($60,000)	$5,100
T	($50,000)	$4,200
U	($30,000)	$6,800
V	($10,000)	$2,000

Table 6.2. Choice of Projects Based on Highest NPV

Project	Initial cash outlay ($)	NPV ($)	Amount spent ($)
P	($20,000)	$8,000	$20,000
Q	($70,000)	$7,200	$90,000
U	($30,000)	$6,800	$120,000
R	($40,000)	$6,500	$160,000
S	($60,000)	$5,100	$220,000

However, this is not the correct approach to take in solving capital rationing problems. Instead, we should maximize the NPV in terms of the relevant constraint (i.e., capital). This is achieved by calculating the profitability index (PI) using the equation PI = NPV/initial cost.

Table 6.3 shows the results for the projects under consideration.

The projects are then ranked on the basis of PI (see Table 6.4).

The optimal combination using the PI is P, U, V, R, Q, and 50% of project S ($30,000/60,000), which provides a total NPV of $33,050, which exceeds the previous combination by $1,150 or 3.6%.

Table 6.3. Calculation of PI

Project	Initial cash outlay ($)	PI
P	(20,000)	0.4
Q	($70,000)	0.103
R	($40,000)	0.1625
S	($60,000)	0.085
T	($50,000)	0.084
U	($30,000)	0.227
V	($10,000)	0.2

Table 6.4. Choice of Projects Based on Highest PI

Project	PI	Initial cash outlay ($)	Amount spent ($)
P	0.4	($20,000)	$20,000
U	0.227	($30,000)	$50,000
V	0.2	($10,000)	$60,000
R	0.1625	($40,000)	$100,000
Q	0.103	($70,000)	$170,000
S	0.085	($60,000)	$230,000

Mutually Exclusive Projects

If two of the projects under consideration are mutually exclusive, then a similar process is carried out by ranking the projects on the basis of PI. It is then necessary to establish two groups, each of which contains one of the mutually exclusive projects. For example, in the group of projects previously considered, if projects P and U were mutually exclusive, then the two groups would be (P, Q, R, S, T, and V) and (Q, R, S, T, U, and V). We would then proceed as before (see tables 6.5 and 6.6).

The optimum NPV from Group 1 is $28,800 (projects P, V, R, Q, and S), while the optimum NPV from Group 2 is $26,750 (projects U, V, R, Q, and 5/6 S). Therefore, the optimum combination is chosen from Group 1 on the basis of superior NPV. It is evident that the mutual exclusivity of the two most attractive projects in the group considerably reduces the NPV from that previously attainable ($33,050).

Table 6.5. Group 1

Project	PI	Initial cash outlay ($)	Amount spent ($)
P	0.4	($20,000)	$20,000
V	0.20	($10,000)	$30,000
R	0.1625	($40,000)	$70,000
Q	0.103	($70,000)	$140,000
S	0.085	($60,000)	$200,000

Table 6.6. Group 2

Project	PI	Initial cash outlay ($)	Amount spent ($)
U	0.227	($30,000)	$30,000
V	0.20	($10,000)	$40,000
R	0.1625	($40,000)	$80,000
Q	0.103	($70,000)	$150,000
S	0.085	($60,000)	$210,000

Multiperiod Capital Rationing

If we extend single-period capital rationing to cover more than one period, then the problem becomes more complex. In such circumstances, we cannot proceed by simply ranking the projects on the basis of PI, as we did with the single period constraint. This is because we now face multiple constraints (one for each period), as opposed to the single constraint encountered previously. To solve these constraints simultaneously, we need to use the optimizing technique of linear programming.

The objective of maximizing shareholder wealth remains the same, but we formulate an objective function using the estimated NPVs for each project. That is,

objective function

$$\text{Max } NPVaA + NPVbB + NPVcC + NPVdD,$$

where NPVa, NPVb, NPVc, and NPVd are the NPVs of the projects and A, B, C, and D are the proportions of the projects invested in.

The next stage is to set up a constraint for each period (clearly some or all of the projects will involve net cash outflows in future periods for such a problem to exist). If, for example, we have capital constraints for three periods, then there will be three constraints:

$$CoA + CoB + CoC + CoD < X \text{ (period 0)}$$

$$CoA + CoB + CoC + CoD < Y \text{ (period 1)}$$

$$CoA + CoB + CoC + CoD < Z \text{ (period 2)}$$

where CoA, CoB, CoC, and CoD are the cash outflows for projects A, B, C, and D, and X, Y, and Z are the capital constraints for periods 0, 1, and 2.

The linear programming problem will usually be solved by the simplex method, using computer software that will calculate the optimal combination of the four projects that will maximize contribution. In addition, other output will include dual values (shadow prices) for each of the capital constraints, which will indicate the amount by which the overall NPV could be increased by relaxing the capital constraints by one unit.

The use of linear programming involves various assumptions, including that the projects are infinitely divisible. If this is not realistic, then the more complex technique of integer programming could be employed. Perhaps the most serious drawback of linear programming is not having any satisfactory method of adjusting the technique to account for risk.

Survey Evidence

Very few studies focus exclusively on capital rationing, though some evidence has been forthcoming from studies examining the capital budgeting process. Earlier studies from the mid-1970s suggest that between 50% and 75% of firms operate under a capital constraint, with limits on borrowing as the primary cause.[1]

A more recent study does focus on capital rationing within the Fortune 500 companies.[2] Of the respondents, 64% operate under a capital rationing environment at least part of the time, which is in line with the previous studies. This is exclusively soft rationing for the larger companies, but for 25% of the smallest companies it is externally imposed. The primary determinant of the investment ceiling was closely tied to the level of internally generated funds, though there was a willingness to raise the ceiling to accommodate high NPV projects, which suggested the capital rationing is predominantly soft in nature. The overall conclusion was that the primary motive underlying capital rationing was a reluctance to issue external finance.

While most of the previous evidence tends to suggest that the capital rationing identified is predominantly of the soft category, the ongoing global credit crisis provides an opportunity to study the effects of financial constraints (liquidity) on real corporate actions. A survey of 1,050 CFOs in the United States, Europe, and Asia attempted to directly assess whether their firms are financially constrained.[3] It was subsequently revealed that 86% of the financially constrained firms in the United States indicate that their ability to currently invest in positive NPV projects is limited by their ability to raise external finance in the capital markets (similar results are found for Europe and Asia). In addition, 56% of these companies in the United States indicate they would cancel investment when external funding is limited (the figure for Europe is 69%). Clearly, the credit crisis of 2008–2009 has systematically impacted real investment among financially constrained companies (as well as burning cash, reducing dividend payments, and engaging in asset sales), which also has implications for the speed of recovery from the current economic downturn.

CHAPTER 7

Replacement Decisions and Lease Versus Buy Decisions

Two variations on the typical investment decision are the replacement decision and the lease versus buy decision, though the latter could arguably be classified as a financing, rather than investment, decision. However, for many smaller companies leasing provides an alternative method of financing an asset where the capital cost may otherwise be prohibitive. Similarly, certain industry sectors, such as the airline industry, rely heavily on lease finance.

A replacement decision may warrant consideration when improvements in technology offer either production cost reductions or enhancements to the product itself. The latter are usually driven by R and D investments and do not significantly impact the balance sheet, whereas the former invariably involve expenditure on sophisticated new machinery and do exert a significant impact on the balance sheet of the company.

An alternative category of replacement decision occurs when assets are replaced on a recurring basis, not necessarily as a consequence of technological advancement. Common types of assets where such decisions are typical include cars, computers, and smaller items of machinery and equipment.

In summary, the following are the two questions that need to be evaluated with respect to replacement decisions:

1. Should the existing equipment be replaced?
2. What should be the replacement policy for assets replaced on a recurring basis?

The first question is addressed by assessing the potential benefits and costs associated with replacing the current asset with a new asset that benefits from improved technology. The improvements may manifest themselves in terms of reduced material requirements, improved labor efficiency, or both.

Example 7.1

Nevis Ltd. manufactures a thermostat that can be used in a variety of kitchen appliances. The current manufacturing process is semiautomated and uses equipment that costs $540,000 and has a written-down value of $300,000. Demand for the thermostat has been relatively stable for the past few years at a level of 50,000 units per year.

Although the existing equipment is expected to have an economic life of 4 more years before being sold for an estimated $40,000, the company is considering the purchase of new equipment that would completely automate the production process. The new equipment would cost $650,000 and also have an expected life of 4 years, after which it could be sold for an estimated $170,000. If the new equipment was purchased, the old equipment could be sold immediately for 50% of its book value.

The finance director has estimated that the variable costs of producing the thermostat would change as a consequence of the improved production process (see Table 7.1). Nevis Ltd. has a cost of capital of 12% per annum.

Solution

From the variable cost estimates, the cost saved per unit from introducing the fully automated process amounts to $2.75 per unit, mainly due to a considerable reduction in labor costs. Assuming current demand is maintained, the annual savings are the following:

Table 7.1. Variable Cost per Unit

	Current ($)	New equipment ($)
Materials	3.65	3.20
Labor	3.30	1.20
Other variable costs	1.60	1.40
	8.55	5.80

Annual savings = $2.75 × 50,000 = $137,500

The initial capital cost is $650,000 minus the $150,000 received from the sale of the existing machinery, resulting in a net outlay of $500,000. A residual value of $170,000 is expected from the sale of the new equipment after 4 years of use.

The net present value (NPV) of the proposal is therefore

NPV = (500,000) + 137,500(3.037) + 170,000(0.636) = $25,708.

On the basis of these calculations, the proposal would appear acceptable.

Perhaps the more typical replacement problem is the second scenario, in which the asset in question is replaced by a similar asset on a regular cycle. In such circumstances there are arguments in favor of replacing the asset earlier:

- Lower maintenance costs
- Higher disposal value
- Higher quality output and service

The main argument against replacing the asset earlier is the associated capital cost. The problem to be solved in this case is to identify the optimum replacement cycle, taking into account the increasing costs of retention against the capital cost of replacement. Where a project forms part of a continuous replacement cycle, the NPV rule requires modification with a choice of three basic methods for determining the optimum replacement cycle:

- Lowest common multiple method
- Finite horizon method
- Equivalent annual cost (EAC) method

Example 7.2

Blackthorn Ltd. operates a machine that has the operating costs and residual values over its 3-year life shown in Table 7.2.

The purchase cost of the machine is $25,000 and the company's cost of capital is 10%.

Table 7.2. Annual Operating Costs and Resale Values

	Year 1	Year 2	Year 3
Operating costs ($)	7,500	10,000	12,500
End-of-year resale value ($)	15,000	10,000	7,500

Replacements are continuous and are assumed to occur into the indefinite future. The following are the replacement options:

- Every year
- Every 2 years
- Every 3 years (at end of useful life)

To compare these options, it is necessary to assess the costs over a comparable period of time.

Method 1: Lowest Common Multiple Method

The cash flows are estimated over a period of time that is the lowest common multiple of all the replacement cycles being considered. In the previous example, the lowest common multiple is 6 years, which results in six 1-year cycles, three 2-year cycles, and two 3-year cycles. The cash flows are then discounted for each option over the time period, and the option with the lowest present value of cost is chosen (see tables 7.3–7.5).

The present value of each series of cash flows can then be calculated as shown in Table 7.6.

The optimum replacement policy would be to replace the machinery every 3 years since this cycle has the lowest total present value of costs.

Table 7.3. Option 1: Every Year

Year		$	$
0	Purchase		(25,000)
1–5	Operating cost	(7,500)	
	Resale value	15,000	
	New purchase	(25,000)	(17,500)
6	Operating cost	(7,500)	
	Resale value	15,000	7,500

Table 7.4. Option 2: Every 2 Years

Year		$	$
0	Purchase		(25,000)
1	Operating cost		(7,500)
2	Operating cost	(10,000)	
	Resale value	10,000	
	New purchase	(25,000)	(25,000)
3, 5	Same as year 1		(7,500)
4	Same as year 2		(25,000)
6	Operating cost	(10,000)	
	Resale value	10,000	0

Table 7.5. Option 3: Every 3 Years

Year		$	$
0	Purchase		(25,000)
1	Operating cost		(7,500)
2	Operating cost		(10,000)
3	Operating cost	(12,500)	
	Resale value	7,500	
	New purchase	(25,000)	(30,000)
4	Same as year 1		(7,500)
5	Same as year 2		(10,000)
6	Operating cost	(12,500)	
	Resale value	7,500	(5,000)

Table 7.6. Summary of Present Values of Replacement Options

Replacement cycle	Present value $ (@ 10%)
Every year	(87,097)
Every two years	(79,834)
Every three years	(76,761)

Method 2: The Finite Horizon Method

The lowest common multiple method is relatively straightforward when the maximum life of the asset is comparatively short, as shown in example 7.2. However, it becomes long and tedious for assets with longer lives; for example, if the maximum life was 5 years, then the lowest common multiple would be 60 years. The finite horizon method calculates the present value of costs over a "significant" time period—say, 20 years—since the present value of cash flows beyond this time is unlikely to have much impact on the relative costs of the replacement options. This method is therefore an approximation method with the expectation that the result will still be the same.

Method 3: The EAC Method

The quickest method of establishing the optimum replacement cycle is the EAC method because the present value of costs is calculated for only one cycle of each of the replacement options. For our previous example the results are displayed in Table 7.7.

Clearly, the present values in Table 7.7 would not be comparable since they relate to different time periods during which replacement is continuous. The solution is to calculate an annuity (EAC) that has the same present value as the cost of repeated cycles of the time periods being considered. That is,

EAC = present value of cost over one replacement cycle/Annuity factor for number of years in cycle.

For our example, the calculations can be found in Table 7.8.

Table 7.7. Present Values for One Cycle of Replacement Options

Year	Annual ($)	Present value ($)	Every 2 years ($)	Present value ($)	Every 3 years ($)	Present value ($)
0	(25,000)	(25,000)	(25,000)	(25,000)	(25,000)	(25,000)
1	7,500	6,818	(7,500)	(6,818)	(7,500)	(6,818)
2			0	0	(10,000)	(8,260)
3					(5,000)	(3,755)
Total		(18,182)		(31,818)		(43,833)

Table 7.8. Calculation of EAC

Cycle	Present value ($)	Annuity factor (10%)	EAC ($)
Every year	(18,182)	0.909	(20,002)
Every 2 years	(31,818)	1.736	(18,328)
Every 3 years	(43,833)	2.487	(17,625)

The interpretation of these results implies that, under the 3-year replacement cycle, the various costs associated with purchasing, operating, and selling the machine over the 3-year period equate to an EAC of $17,625, which is the lowest of the three options.

In general, the EAC method is the preferred method, though the choice is less obvious with the presence of inflation. If there is a single rate of inflation, we can proceed without inflating the cash flows over one cycle of the alternative replacement options and then divide by the "real" rate annuity factor. That is,

EAC = present value of uninflated cost over one replacement cycle/ Real rate annuity.

In the event of multiple rates of inflation, the lowest common multiple method would appear preferable. The cash flows over the entire lowest common multiple period would be inflated using the different rates of inflation and then discounted using the nominal (monetary) discount rate.

Example 7.3

Boston Bakers are considering the replacement policy for their baking ovens. The ovens are heavily used and the choice is between replacing every 2 years or every 3 years. The ovens costs $24,500 each and have the maintenance costs and resale values shown in Table 7.9.

The original cost, maintenance cost, and resale values are expressed in current prices. The finance director is unsure about inflation rates during the period under consideration and is considering two alternative assumptions:

Table 7.9. Maintenance Costs and Resale Values

Year	Maintenance costs ($)	Resale value ($)
1	500	
2	800	15,600
3	1,500	11,200

1. All costs will increase at a rate of 6.5% per annum and the company's nominal discount rate is 16% (tables 7.10 and 7.11).
2. The maintenance costs will increase at 10% per annum and oven replacement and resale values will increase at 5% per annum. The company's nominal discount rate is 15% (tables 7.12–7.15).

Scenario 1

The monetary discount rate is 15% and the inflation rate is 6.5%; therefore, the real discount rate can be calculated in the following way:

Table 7.10. Two-Year Replacement

Year	Cost ($)	Maintenance ($)	Resale ($)	Cash flow ($)	DCF @ 8%	Present value ($)
0	(24,500)			(24,500)	1.000	(24,500)
1		(500)		(500)	0.926	(463)
2		(800)	15,600	14,800	0.857	12,684
NPV						(12,279)

Table 7.11. Three-Year Replacement

Year	Cost ($)	Maintenance ($)	Resale ($)	Cash flow ($)	DCF @ 8%	Present value ($)
0	(24,500)			(24,500)	1.000	(24,500)
1		(500)		(500)	0.926	(463)
2		(800)		(800)	0.857	(686)
3		(1,500)	11,200	9,700	0.794	7,702
NPV						(17,947)

Table 7.12. Two-Year Replacement

Year	Cost ($)	Maintenance ($)	Resale ($)	Cash flow ($)
0	(24,500)*			(24,500)
1		$500 \times 1.1 = (550)$		(550)
2	(27,011)*	$800 \times 1.1^2 = (968)$	17,199*	(10,780)
3		$500 \times 1.1^3 = (666)$		(666)
4	(29,780)*	$800 \times 1.1^4 = (1,171)$	18,962*	(11,989)
5		$500 \times 1.1^5 = (805)$		(805)
6		$800 \times 1.1^6 = (1,417)$	20,905*	19,488

* The initial cost of $24,500 and resale value of $15,600 are inflated at 5% to provide the figures for years 2, 4, and 6.

Table 7.13. Present Value of Two-Year Replacement

Year	Cash flow ($)	DCF @ 15%	Present value ($)
0	(24,500)	1.000	(24,500)
1	(55)	0.870	(479)
2	(10,780)	0.756	(8,150)
3	(666)	0.658	(438)
4	(11,989)	0.572	(6,858)
5	(805)	0.497	(400)
6	19,488	0.432	8,419
NPV			(32,406)

Table 7.14. Three-Year Replacement

Year	Cost ($)	Maintenance ($)	Resale ($)	Cash flow ($)
0	(24,500)*			(24,500)
1		$500 \times 1.1 = (550)$		(550)
2	(28,362)*	$800 \times 1.1^2 = (968)$		(968)
3		$1,500 \times 1.1^3 = (1,997)$	12,965*	(17,394)
4		$500 \times 1.1^4 = (732)$		(732)
5		$800 \times 1.1^5 = (1,288)$		(1,288)
6		$1,500 \times 1.1^6 = (2,657)$	15,009*	12,352

* The initial cost of $24,500 and resale value of $11,200 are inflated at 5% to provide the figures for years 2, 3, and 6.

Table 7.15. Present Value of Three-Year Replacement

Year	Cash flow ($)	DCF @ 15%	Present value ($)
0	(24,500)	1.000	(24,500)
1	(550)	0.870	(479)
2	(968)	0.756	(732)
3	(17,394)	0.658	(11,445)
4	(732)	0.572	(419)
5	(1,288)	0.497	(640)
6	12,352	0.432	5,336
NPV			(32,879)

$$(1 + \text{nominal rate}) = (1 + \text{real rate})(1 + \text{inflation rate})$$

$$1.15 = (1 + \text{real rate})(1.065)$$

$$\text{real rate} = (1.15/1.065) - 1 = 0.08 = 8\%$$

Unadjusted cash flows are discounted above at 8% and the present values divided by the relevant 8% annuity factor to give the following results:

$$\text{EAC (2-year replacement)} = \$12,279/1.783 = \$6,887$$

$$\text{EAC (3-year replacement)} = \$17,947/2.577 = \$6,984$$

The recommendation is therefore the 2-year replacement cycle with a slightly lower equivalent annual cost.

Scenario 2

The recommendation is therefore the 2-year replacement cycle with a slightly lower net present cost.

Lease Versus Buy Decisions

Once an investment decision has been made to proceed with the acquisition of an asset, the means of financing the purchase cost require consideration. For some companies, leasing may provide a means of accessing the capital markets when loan financing is difficult to obtain. Even when financing is available, there may be some attraction in avoiding the need for a substantial capital outlay at the start of a project.

The International Accounting Standards Board (IASB) defines a lease in the following terms: "A leasing transaction is a commercial arrangement whereby an equipment owner conveys the right to use the equipment in return for payment by the equipment user of a specified rental over a pre-agreed period of time."[1]

Leasing bears strong similarities to both using an installment plan and borrowing, and as a consequence, it is often undertaken by banks and similar institutions. Some manufacturing companies also operate leasing subsidiaries as a vehicle for marketing their own products, IBM and John Deere being notable examples. Various types of lease are available, with the length of time for which the asset is required being one of the main distinguishing features. If the lessee (user) of the asset only wishes to use the equipment for a specific job (e.g., oil well drilling or a construction project), then a short-term or "operating" lease is appropriate. The asset is then returned to the lessor, who bears the risk of downtime before another user requires the asset.

For our purposes, the long-term or "finance" lease is of more relevance when the lessee requires use of the asset for most of its expected useful life. When the lease expires, the parties may negotiate a secondary lease or the lessee may have an option to purchase the asset. The classification of a lease as either operating or finance also brings up associated issues regarding the differing accounting treatments. In broad terms, finance leases must now be capitalized on the balance sheet, whereas operating leases do not bring this obligation. Originally, the absence of any accounting disclosure allowed finance leases to be disguised as "off-balance" sheet finance, which, in turn, understated borrowing with associated difficulties with estimating gearing ratios. The IASB is currently examining the feasibility of aligning the accounting treatment of finance and operating leases to require all leases to be disclosed on the balance sheet.

To evaluate the lease option against the purchase option, we can proceed by performing a present value analysis based on the following respective cash flows:

1. Purchase option
   - Initial capital cost
   - Benefit of tax depreciation allowance

- Operating and maintenance cost
- Residual value

2. Lease option
   - Lease payment to lessor
   - Tax saving on lease payment

Example 7.4

Sorrell Plc is considering whether to purchase or lease new technology equipment at a cost to buy of $100,000. The equipment will have a productive life of 5 years, after which it will have no residual value. If purchased, there will be a $2,000 maintenance cost. With the lease option, an annual payment of $25,000 is inclusive of the maintenance costs.

The finance director estimates Sorrell's cost of capital to be 18% per annum and its pretax cost of debt to be 14%. If the equipment is purchased, 25% tax depreciation allowances are available and the company's relevant rate of corporation tax is 30%.

Solution

The outcome of the decision is that the leasing option is more financially attractive on the basis of a lower negative net present value (see tables 7.16–7.18). It should also be noted that the discount rate used for the calculations was the after-tax cost of debt of 10% (14%(1–0.3)) rather than the company's cost of capital. The rationale for this discount rate is that we are considering a financing decision, as opposed to an investment

Table 7.16. Tax Benefits

Year	Tax depreciation	Tax savings (@ 30%)	Tax savings on maintenance costs	Total tax benefits
1	25,000	7,500	600	8,100
2	18,750	5,625	600	6,225
3	14,063	4,219	600	4,819
4	10,547	3,164	600	3,764
5	31,640	9,492	600	10,092

Table 7.17. Present Value of Purchase Option

Year	Initial cost	Maintenance	Tax savings	Cash flow	Present value
0	(100,000)			(100,000)	(100,000)
1		(2,000)		(2,000)	(1,818)
2		(2,000)	8,100	6,100	5,039
3		(2,000)	6,225	4,225	3,173
4		(2,000)	4,819	2,819	1,925
5		(2,000)	3,764	1,764	1,095
6			10,092	10,092	5,702
Present Value					(84,884)

Table 7.18. Present Value of Lease Option

Year	Lease payments	Tax saving	Annuity factor	Present value
1–5	(25,000)		3.791	(94,775)
2–6		7,500	3.446	25,845
Present value				(68,930)

decision, for which the cost of capital would have been utilized. Similarly, due to borrowing to finance the acquisition of the asset, it is the posttax cost of debt that is the appropriate discount rate.

In example 7.4, we have implicitly assumed the acceptability of the equipment purchase from an investment perspective and merely considered the lease or purchase decision as a financing decision. An alternative approach is to combine the two decisions, investment and financing, into an adjusted present value calculation. There is a possibility that a project exhibiting a negative net present value as an investment may prove attractive when the present value of the financing option is incorporated.

Advantages of Leasing

1. The most obvious benefit associated with leasing is in terms of cash flow by avoiding a significant capital cost to purchase the asset. It should, however, be remembered that an initial advance payment of 3 to 6 months of lease payments is commonly required. In addition, the fixed nature of lease payments facilitates cash planning.
2. A finance lease may be cheaper than the equivalent loan, and the tax benefits also help to alleviate the cost.
3. The finance charge elements of a finance lease are tax deductable.
4. The differing types of lease available offer the potential lessee considerable flexibility in financing arrangements.
5. Lease finance is easily available and is less restrictive than many sources of finance.
6. No security is necessary to cover the finance raised as the leased asset itself provides security.

Disadvantages of Leasing

The main potential drawback of leasing is that it may be difficult, or at least very expensive, to cancel leases if business conditions change and the asset is no longer required.

The Impact of the Economic Downturn on Leasing

Recent figures appear to suggest that, in line with significant decreases in capital expenditure, the leasing industry has also suffered from the ongoing impact of the recent economic downturn. The Equipment Leasing and Finance Association[2] in the United States reports that overall new business volume for October 2009 declined by 32.8% compared to the same period in 2008. In addition, the volume of new business decreased by 23% from July to August 2009. In the United Kingdom, the Finance and Leasing Association[3] reported a 26% decline in new business for July 2009 compared to July 2008, though this was the smallest rate of contraction in new business since March 2009.

CHAPTER 8

Strategic Investment Decisions

Capital investment can range from relatively small operational projects consisting of expenditure on new or replacement equipment to substantial investments, which have a more "strategic" focus with a potentially significant impact on long-term corporate performance. Typical examples of the latter include the introduction of new technology, the introduction of major new product lines, and, perhaps most significantly, the acquisition of, or merger with, other companies. The distinguishing features of strategic, as opposed to operational, investments relate to the higher risks and expenditure involved with the increased complexity associated with identifying the potential outcomes. As a consequence of the latter feature, such projects present particular challenges in the evaluation process.

Clearly, capital investment must be viewed as an integral component of the strategic decision-making activity of an organization. As with other strategic decisions, capital investment must respond to changes in technology and the environment in addition to long-term strategic direction. Such variables often rest uneasily within quantitative decision models due to their nebulous and uncertain nature. Consequently, the applicability of discounted cash flow models, which tend to be biased toward short-term, less strategic investments, has been called into question. Furthermore, such techniques are inadequate for capturing the intangible attributes of strategic projects and fail to encapsulate the value of future flexibility inherent in many investments of this nature.

As a consequence of the implied failings of conventional financial analysis, it has been argued that strategic investment projects should not be evaluated solely on the basis of generating economic value. Instead, a complementary evaluation of their potential contribution to competitive strategy would appear appropriate, incorporating variables such as product quality, strategic fit, and improved competitive position. Such intangible benefits are generally difficult to quantify using conventional financial techniques, suggesting that an alternative approach may be necessary. Indeed, it would appear that a more sophisticated approach integrating both strategic and financial considerations into the analysis of strategic projects might alleviate the inadequacies and incompleteness of discounted cash flow analysis.

After examining the strategic investment decision in more depth, we shall identify a number of the emergent techniques available that attempt to encapsulate both quantitative and qualitative factors and that have been linked with strategic capital investment decision making. A brief description of each of the techniques will be followed by an assessment of their potential for assessing strategic investment projects. In closing, empirical evidence regarding the use of both conventional financial analysis and the emergent techniques in evaluating strategic investment projects will be summarized and discussed.

The term "strategic investment decision" is often viewed as a somewhat nebulous concept, drawing from the finance, management accounting, and strategic management literatures. A particular problem results from the distinctive approaches to understanding and improving investment decision making promoted across these disciplines. Finance is characterized by a theoretical economic approach, management accounting by case study observations, and strategic management by a qualitative-strategic approach. The management problem is to evaluate the strategic fit of the project, whereas the financial problem is to evaluate the likely outcome prior to committing significant financial resources to the project. The typical strategic investment decision involves so many complexities and uncertainties that it is almost inevitably more qualitative than quantitative. Moreover, in an organizational context, the strategic investment decision potentially involves many managers of differing degrees of seniority, functional experience, and industry-specific knowledge. Consequently, many view strategic investment decision making as a sociopolitical process, with a requirement for management to reach agreement or consensus on the decision.

Recently, a major research project has been published in the United Kingdom by the Chartered Institute of Management Accountants.[1]

Based largely on a survey of the existing literature, a 10-stage process for making strategic investment decisions is proposed:

1. Scanning for project opportunities
2. Definition of potential projects and formulation of strategic options
3. Generation of project data
4. Making preliminary assumptions and sketching the project profile
5. Early screening to establish if the idea is to be progressed
6. Estimation of financial data using more specific assumptions
7. Formal evaluation using DCF techniques
8. Progression through company gathering support and culminating with submission at board level
9. Project authorization at board level
10. Postaudit evaluation

Clearly, the application of project appraisal techniques accounts for only one stage in the process, and the study attempts to explore the role of both individual and collective managerial judgment rather than focusing on how individuals make decisions.

The study proceeds to carry out a cross-sectional study of senior management accountants, which provided the overriding impression that both formal and psychological judgments are exercised in the process. It is suggested that management accounting textbooks need to acknowledge the context in which strategic investment decisions are made, as well as the impact of human behavior on decisions, rather than focusing purely on the analytical skills. In particular, decision makers at this level require competency in the "softer skills," including negotiating, sharing information, and reaching a consensus.

The Emergent Techniques

The Balanced Scorecard

Perhaps the most notable attempt to combine both financial and non-financial performance measures to give management a comprehensive overview of the business was devised in the early 1990s.[2] The underlying objective was to move away from an almost exclusive reliance on financial performance measures, which were criticized as being, inter alia, inconsistent with modern business reality, backward looking, and irrelevant to many parts of the organization. The nonfinancial performance measures were identified as three perspectives related to the customer, the internal business, and innovation and learning. The financial perspective remains, but primarily as confirmation that the strategy executed for the other perspectives is having an impact on the organization's financial returns. Indeed, most scorecard users continue to consider financial performance measures as the most important component of the scorecard.

While the balanced scorecard was perhaps initially viewed as a measurement system, it has evolved into a crucial tool for aligning short-term actions with long-term strategy. The outcomes of the scorecard performance measures provide an indication of how successfully strategy has been achieved. It has been suggested that the innovation and learning perspective is the driving force behind the other perspectives, ultimately leading to financial returns. Innovation is a multidimensional, complex activity that many firms find difficult to articulate in terms of identifying appropriate metrics for the innovation and learning perspective. However, metrics for innovation are crucial to justify investments of this type, which are typically long-term, risky projects that create more intangible than tangible value. Without such metrics, it follows that investment decisions are largely intuitive, with the estimation of value creation similarly problematic.

Therefore, strategic investment decisions ideally should be accommodated within the framework of the balanced scorecard, which clearly defines strategic objectives. The scorecard can then be utilized to evaluate strategic investment proposals and ensure such proposals are aligned with corporate strategy. In addition, appropriate metrics are instrumental in understanding the sources of value and, in turn, measuring the value created by projects.

Real Options

An extensive literature has developed around the application of financial option valuation techniques to strategic investment decisions. A financial option is an option to buy (call) or sell (put) a financial asset that already exists and is actively traded on a financial market in a standard form. Essentially, they allow the holder of the option to take a view on the future price of the underlying asset and profit from movements in the price of that asset without incurring the larger capital outlay of purchasing the assets outright. In contrast, a real option is an option to alter the "real" physical or intellectual activity of a business by creating a new factory, a new brand, or even a new technology.

A number of option valuation techniques are available for financial options, although the Black-Scholes equation tends to dominate the literature. In this model, five variables influence the value of the option: namely, the market price of the underlying asset, the exercise price at which the holder is given the right to buy or sell the underlying asset, the time period until the option expires, the risk-free rate of return, and the volatility of asset price. These five variables exert varying influences on the value of the option.

Contemporary corporate project appraisal techniques treat capital projects as if they are financial instruments, such as shares or bonds. Indeed, net present value (NPV) was initially developed to value one-off, passive investment strategies such as whether to invest in bonds, but was subsequently applied to project valuation. Consequently, NPV is a one-off decision and implies that investment plans are not modified regardless of how conditions change. In reality, managers can observe the accuracy of their forecasts along with competitor reactions and market characteristics. If necessary, they can make a strategic decision to increase or decrease the size of the investment, or even abandon it if appropriate (i.e., real options). Conventional discounted cash flow analysis does not lend itself to estimating the correct value of flexible projects, because it does not provide the methodology for measuring the value of real options, which offer flexibility.

Real options analysis enables an integration of decisions on investment, operations, and disinvestment and follows the understanding that at least one of the value determining variables is evolving in an unpredictable manner, but there is flexibility in responding to the uncertainty as it unfolds. We shall return to real options in a later chapter and investigate the alternative valuation techniques available with a more detailed discussion of the scenarios to which it has been applied.

Technology Roadmapping

The issue of technology management is becoming increasingly important and critical in delivering competitive advantage to companies. However, previously there was a lack of effective processes to manage technology, which resulted in many technological investment projects, such as robotics, computer integrated manufacturing, and flexible manufacturing systems, failing.[3] The failure was not due to the technology itself, but to the fact that the links between technology and the strategy to satisfy the business needs were not well understood. As a result, companies today are aware of the importance of technology strategy and are concerned about how to deploy and manage technology to support the goals of the business. Clearly, there is a need to understand the potential of existing and new technologies and to integrate and exploit them to provide new capabilities, products, and processes in the context of business and corporate strategy.[4] The effective management of technology in both explicit and tacit technological knowledge requires appropriate methods or systems, such as a technology roadmap process that can support the development and implementation of integrated strategic business, product, and technology plans.

A technology roadmap is a plan that matches short-term and long-term goals with specific technology solutions to help meet those goals. It has been described as "a process that contributes . . . to the definition of technology strategy by displaying the interaction between products and technologies over time"[5] by using charts and graphs to reveal the links between technology and business needs. It links the strategic vision and intent of an enterprise with its product, process, and technology and innovations. Roadmapping can be customized at different levels—product, enterprise, industry, economy, or the world.[6]

Developing a roadmap has three major uses.[7] It helps reach a consensus about a set of needs and the technologies required to satisfy those needs, it provides a mechanism to help forecast technology developments, and it provides a framework to help plan and coordinate technology developments. A key aim of technology roadmapping is to look both within and beyond the firm to ensure that the right capabilities are in place, at the right time, to achieve strategic objectives. Technology roadmapping, therefore, has obvious potential to be applied to strategic investment decision making. The following is advocated:

> Technology roadmap can be used to ensure that investments in assets such as new fabrication processes, products and factory layouts, made by different subunits of the firm, are coordinated with one another and with investments in enabling and related technologies made by other firms. . . . The requirement that investments be consistent with a technology roadmap means that proponents of individual investments have to ensure that their proposals synchronise and fit with related investments taking place within and beyond the firm in a manner that enhances value.[8]

It was found from case studies of four different technology roadmaps that the upper strategic element of a technology roadmap usually receives much less attention than its lower operational capabilities counterpart. More research is therefore recommended to better integrate the strategic drivers in future technology roadmaps.

Value Chain Analysis

In 1985, a generic value chain model comprising a sequence of activities found to be common to a wide range of firms was introduced.[9] This comprised the linked set of value-creating activities from the basic raw materials through component suppliers to the ultimate product delivered to the customers.

Value chain analysis is a strategic analysis tool that can assist in assessing a company's competitive advantage, identifying where value to customers can be increased or costs reduced, and providing an improved understanding of the company's linkage with suppliers, customers, and competitors. In 1989, value chain analysis was blended with cost driver analysis and competitive value analysis to form the strategic cost management (SCM) framework.[10] However, strictly speaking, Shanks's strategic analysis tools equate to a thorough application of value chain analysis as described by Porter.

The underlying concept of value chain analysis is that each individual company occupies a selected part, or parts, of the entire value chain. The part or parts to occupy are selected by a strategic analysis of competitive advantage, that is, where value can be provided to the customer at the lowest possible cost. For example, in the oil and gas industry, companies may operate upstream in geotech analysis, exploration, or production or downstream in refining, transport, or distribution. Similarly, in the computer manufacturing industry, some companies primarily manufacture components (chips, hard drives, monitors) whereas others combine manufactured and purchased components to manufacture the finished computer.

A distinction can be made between internal and external value chains, with the former describing the value-added stages within a company and the latter the value-added stages within an industry. Although the external value chain consists of processes outside the company, it often reveals strategic opportunities including, inter alia, outsourcing, vertical integration, horizontal expansion, and strategic alliances with suppliers. A recent contribution[11] suggests applying value chain analysis to discover the strategic requirements of important customers. Such an approach should assist suppliers in distinguishing between the activities of the customer that directly support its competitive strategies and routine operations offering little scope for competitive advantage. Not only will this enhance relationships with suppliers, but it also assists in the identification of high-value new business opportunities, offering the potential for future profits.

A criticism of conventional capital budgeting techniques is a failure to provide a complete analysis in the modern competitive environment typified by rapidly changing markets and technology. A company's activities can create value for the entire value chain, even though it participates in only a small segment of the chain. Consequently, a company should analyze the potential impact of its capital investments over the entire value chain. The potential significance of this approach was demonstrated by a field analysis of a company that initially performed a conventional capital budgeting analysis that considered only operational benefits within the company itself.[12] This analysis recommended that the proposed investment should not proceed, but a value chain analysis that considered the impact on both upstream and downstream operations was subsequently undertaken. This revealed potential annual savings of $33.6 million on just one of the company's locations, and the decision was reversed.

Benchmarking

Benchmarking has been defined as "a search for industry best practices that lead to superior performance"[13] and is considered an important tool in assisting organizations to, inter alia, "promote competitive awareness . . . link operational tactics to corporate vision and strategy . . . [and] trigger major step changes in business performance."[14] The emphasis on both promoting competitive awareness and linking operations to strategy reveals a strong association with areas that are integral to strategic capital investment.

Benchmarking was originally invented as a formal process by Rank Xerox in the late 1980s while attempting to improve their distribution process[15] and has become widely used as "one of the more popular of management fashions."[16] However, no single benchmarking process has been universally adopted, with a number of benchmarking frameworks being developed. Although different benchmarking frameworks have different numbers of steps, one major similarity between the frameworks is that they can be condensed into the four major elements of the Deming (PDCA) cycle. In this context, PDCA means planning what to do; doing what has been planned; checking results or effects of what has been done; and finally acting upon those results in terms of standardization, further improvement, or feedback.

It has been suggested[17] that the potential application of benchmarking to strategic capital investment lies in its ability to direct attention outside the firm and toward competitors, the "best in class" companies, and innovation.

Survey Evidence

The preceding discussion suggests that traditional capital budgeting techniques appear to provide an incomplete analysis of the complexities of strategic investment decisions. They are criticized as being project oriented, thereby failing to capture the total impact of a capital investment. Moreover, strategic investment decisions are inherently more uncertain, often involving evolving technologies in a rapidly changing environment. As a consequence the evaluation process for such decisions often involves both increased amounts of nonfinancial data and the application of subjective evaluation criteria.

A number of emergent techniques have been proposed in an attempt to more closely integrate strategic and financial considerations into the analysis of strategic projects to alleviate the perceived inadequacies and incompleteness of discounted cash flow analysis. We shall now conclude this chapter by examining the extent to which these emergent techniques have been embraced by companies when encountering investment decisions of a strategic nature.

A major study published in 1996[18] examined the techniques used for financial and strategic analysis by companies operating in the vehicle components sector in the United Kingdom and Germany, though it also included a number of U.S. subsidiaries. The sector chosen offers a wide range of technologies and competitive positions, and value chain issues were found to have been of critical importance. A case study approach was utilized, with 49 companies being interviewed regarding a single strategic investment project undertaken in the late 1980s and early 1990s.

The interviews revealed that around 30% of UK and German companies used DCF techniques when making strategic investment decisions, but only 14% regarded DCF as the key financial measure when assessing strategic investments. In contrast, 69% of UK companies and 52% of German companies regarded payback as the key financial measure, with the requirement for a rapid payback (less than 3 years) being treated much more seriously in the United Kingdom (78% of companies) compared to an average of 5.2 years in Germany. An additional contrast between the two countries was the stronger emphasis placed on nonfinancial considerations by German companies. However, despite this latter finding, only 25% of both German and UK companies made any use of formal strategic planning techniques.

Value chain analysis was virtually never used explicitly in German companies, although the thought processes observed addressed many of the issues raised. It appeared that intimate customer relationships and a determination to predict customer needs was the breeding ground for the bulk of German strategic investments. The study concluded that the most successful companies devoted more attention to value chain and competitive advantage issues than to financial considerations.

More recently, the use of financial analysis for both nonstrategic and strategic investments was examined.[19] For both categories, NPV was the most used analysis technique, with payback ranked second and internal rate of return third for nonstrategic investments, but the order of the latter two techniques was reversed for strategic investments. A similar analysis for incorporating risk revealed a significantly higher usage of some of the risk-adjustment techniques for strategic investments (i.e., risk-adjusted discount rates and cash flows), although there was little difference for the more sophisticated methods (probability analysis, simulation, sensitivity analysis).

The primary focus of the study, however, was an examination of the usage of the emergent techniques discussed earlier in the evaluation of strategic investments (i.e., balanced scorecard, real options, technology roadmapping, value chain analysis, and benchmarking). A questionnaire was sent to 320 large (turnover > $150 million) UK companies, and a response rate of 30.63% was achieved, with the replies revealing significant variability in both the use and perceived importance of the techniques. The most popular technique was benchmarking, with almost 40% of respondents rating it as important or very important for strategic investment decisions. Although benchmarking is a well established practice in many companies, its application to strategic investment projects was a novel finding. Of the other techniques, value chain analysis and the balanced scorecard were both rated as important or very important by around 20% of respondents, with real options and technology roadmapping considered least important for strategic investment decisions. The overriding conclusion of the survey was that, although academics favored their use for strategic investment decisions, the emergent techniques had, to date at least, little impact on strategic investment decision-making practice.

CHAPTER 9

International Capital Budgeting

Introduction

Modern business operates in a global marketplace and companies that limit their operations solely to domestic markets are likely to encounter increasing competition not only from other domestic companies but also from transnational companies. This internationalization of business has largely been brought about by fundamental political, technological, regulatory, and economic changes during the 1980s and 1990s that include the following:

- Massive deregulation in telecommunications, financial services, and airline sectors
- Integration of international capital and financial markets
- Privatizations designed to reduce the public sector
- Rapid advances in information technology including, more recently, the Internet
- The introduction of free market policies by third world countries

Arguably, the most dramatic change in the international economy over recent years has been the emergence of China as a global competitor. In the 25-year period commencing with the economic reforms of 1978, the GDP of China has increased by 700%, making it the fastest growing economy in the world. Since 2002, China has also been the primary destination for foreign direct investment (FDI), attracting in excess of $50 billion annually and proving attractive to around 400 of the 500 largest companies in the world..

The explosive growth in FDI during the past three decades can be seen in Figure 9.1, which shows both the stock and flow on an annual basis. A particularly rapid increase has occurred in the period from 2000–2007, but the recent turmoil in the economic and financial markets has affected investment for 2008 and is expected to have a significantly greater impact in 2009, as evidenced by a recent comment from the *Financial Times*:

> Foreign direct investment is likely to fall around the world this year as the global financial crisis causes companies to draw in their horns, according to data from a United Nations agency. The UN Conference on Trade and Development (Unctad), the single most comprehensive source of FDI data, said that cross-border investment, which dropped sharply last year, would probably slide from $1,700bn in 2008 to less than $1,200bn (€815bn, £730bn) this year. Such a fall would take it back to levels seen five years ago. "Global FDI flows have been severely affected worldwide by the economic and financial crisis," said the agency's annual report

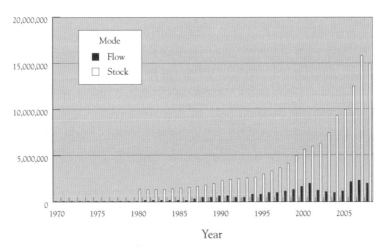

Figure 9.1. Stock and flow of worldwide foreign direct investment: 1980–2008.

Source: UNCTAD World Investment Report 2008 ($ million).

on investment. "The crisis has changed the FDI landscape." (*Financial Times*, Sept 17, 2009)

Prospects for FDI vary significantly by industry, with perhaps the outlook for the service sector being more positive than the manufacturing or primary sectors. Within the sectors, those at the forefront are likely to be information and communication technologies and transportation (service), electrical and electronic products and metals (manufacturing), and mining and petroleum (primary).

Figure 9.2 lists the top 40 of the largest 100 multinationals by the magnitude of their foreign assets. Most of the companies are household names on the basis of their presence in consumer product markets. Of those named, 10 companies are in the motor vehicle sector, and a further 7 companies are involved in the petroleum industry. In terms of country of origin, the United States dominates with 11 companies included, followed by Germany with 8 and Japan with 6.

Motivation for FDI

As with domestic investment projects, companies consider FDI when attempting to improve their profitability and, in turn, enhance shareholder wealth. In the majority of cases, the motivation is either boosting revenues, reducing costs, or both. FDI is usually the final stage of the process of entering into foreign markets, after initially establishing an export market and the interim stage of licensing (the right to use a brand name) when there may be inadequate resources to establish foreign operations. A major factor in the progression through the various stages is the relative cost of each mode of service, which itself is invariably a function of market size or volume of sales. FDI obviously requires the highest commitment of costs to the establishment of production and distribution facilities but avoids the costs of monitoring the licensee to ensure product quality.

A substantial body of literature has built up examining FDI, which has assisted in explaining the dramatic growth in FDI as previously discussed. A useful framework of analysis for summarizing the main motivations underlying FDI identifies three main categories:[1]

Annex table A.I.15. The world's top 100 non-financial TNCs, ranked by foreign assets, 2006[a]
(Millions of dollars and number of employees)

Rankin by: Foreign assets	TNI [b]	II [c]	Corporation	Home economy	Industry [d]	Assets Foreign	Assets Total	Sales Foreign	Sales Total	Employment Foreign	Employment Total
1	71	54	General Eletric	United States	Electrical & electronic equipament	442.278	697.239	74.285	163.391	164.000	319.000
2	14	68	British Petroleum Company Plc	United Kingdom	Petroleum expl./red./distr.	170.326	217.601	215.879	270.602	80.300	97.100
3	87	93	Toyata Motor Corporation	Japan	Motor vehicles	164.627	273.853	78.529	205.918	113.967	299.394
4	34	79	Royla Dutch/Shell Group	United Kingdom, Netherlands	Petroleum expl./red./distr.	161.122*	235.276	182.538*	318.845	90.000	108.000
5	40	35	Exxonmobil Corporation	United States	Petroleum expl./red./distr.	154.993	219.015	363.000	365.467	51.723	82.100
6	78	64	Forda Motor Company	United States	Motor vehicles	131.062	275.554	680.000	160.123	155.000[f]	283.000
7	7	99	Vodafone Group Plc	United Kingdom	Telecommunications	126.19	144.366	78.968	39.021	53.138	63.394
8	26	51	Total	France	Petroleum expl./red./distr.	120.645	138.579	32.641	192.952	57.239	95.070
9	96	36	Electricle De France	France	Electricity, gas and water	111.916	235.857	146.672	73.933	17.185[e]	155.968
10	92	18	Wal-Mart Stores	United States	Ratail	110.199	151.193	33.879	344.992	540.000	1910.000
11	37	34	Telefonic SA	Spain	Telecommunications	101.891	143.530	77.116	66.367	167.881	224.939
12	77	88	E.On	Germany	Electricity, gas and water	94.304	167.565	41.093	85.007	46.598	80.612
13	86	82	Deulsche Telekom AG	Germany	Telecommunications	93.488	171.421	32.154	76.963	88.808	248.800
14	58	65	Volkswagen Group	Germany	Motor vehicles	91.823	179.906	36.240	131.571	155.935	324.875
15	73	57	France Telecom	France	Telecommunications	90.871	135.876	95.761	64.863	82.148	191.036
16	90	63	ConocoPhillips	United States	Petroleum expl./red./distr.	89.528	164.781	30.448	183.650	17.188[g]	38.400
17	56	89	Chevron Corporation	United States	Petroleum expl./red./distr.	85.735	132.628	55.781	204.892	33.700	62.500
18	11	75	Honda Motor Co Ltd	Japan	Motor vehicles	76.264	101.190	111.608	95.333	148.544	167.231
19	36	62	Suez	France	Electricity, gas and water	75.151	96.714	77.605	55.563	76.943	139.814
20	45	48	Siemens AG	Germany	Eletrical & electronic equipament	74.585	119.812	42.002	109.553	314.000	475.000

Ranking by:						Assets		Sales		Employment	
Foreign assets	TNI [b]	II [c]	Corporation	Home economy	Industry [d]	Foreign	Total	Foreign	Total	Foreign	Total
21	10	11	Hutchison Whampoa Limited	Hong Kong, China	Diversified	70.679	87.146	74.858	34.428	182.149*	220.000
22	84	85	RWE Group	Germany	Electricity, gas and water	68.202	123.080	25.619	55.521	30.752	68.534
23	9	7	Nestle SA	Switzerland	Food & beverages	66.677*	83.426	22.142	75.528	247.434*[e]	265.000
24	62	38	BMW AG	Germany	Motor vehicles	66.053	104.118	57.234*	61.472	26.575	106.575
25	51	33	Procter & Gamble	United States	Diversified	64.487	138.014	48.172	76.476	101.220[b]	138.000
26	89	71	General Motors	United States	Motor vehicles	63.538	186.192	44.530	207.349	167.342	280.000
27	48	97	Nissan Motor Co Ltd	Japan	Motor vehicles	61.398	104.264	78.308	90.014	93.935	186.336
28	93	29	Deusche Post AG	Germany	Transport and storafe	60.938	286.709	68.703	75.957	137.251*	463.350
29	72	40	Eri Group	Italy	Petroleum expl./red./distr.	58.113	116.307	44.807	108.023	36.691	73.572
30	50	28	Sanos-avenis	France	Pharmaceuticals	55.342*	102.414	62.429	35.595	71.325	100.289
31	98	70	DaimierChrysler AG	Germany, United States	Motor vehicles	55.214	250.259	20.266*	190.176	98.976	360.385
32	75	49	Pfzer Inc	United States	Pharmaceuticals	53.765	114.837	82.130	48.371	59.818[g]	98.000
33	15	20	Roche Group	Switzerland	Pharmaceuticals	52.178	60.980	22.549	33.531	41.554*	74.372
34	44	72	Mitsui & Co Ltd	Japan	Wholesale trade	50.678	82.499	33.155	41.967	39.792[j]	41.761
35	95	77	Mitsibishi Motors Corporation	Japan	Motor vehicles	48.328	96.559	17.557	176.410	19.048[g]	55.867
36	59	21	IBM	United States	Eletrical & electronic equipament	47.392	103.234	37.270	91.424	231.248	355.766
37	2	15	Xstrata PLC	United Kingdom	Mining & quarrying	45.284	47.216	55.507	17.632	26.506*	28.198
38	49	39	Fiat Spa	Italy	Motor vehicles	44.715	76.785	46.394	65.026	96.261	172.012
39	31	10	Novartis	Switzerland	Pharmaceuticals	42.922	65.008	35.630	36.031	52.830*	100.735
40	52	47	Sony Corporation	Japan	Eletrical & electronic equipament	40.925	98.498	52.045	71.331	103.900	163.000

Figure 9.2. UNCTAD world investment report, 2008.

1. *Strategic motives.* Among the main strategic motivations for FDI would be the following:

- Seeking new markets: Maturing domestic markets characterized by slowing growth and increased competition may encourage an assessment of the potential of foreign markets.
- Sources of raw materials: Many multinationals, particularly oil and mining corporations, invest abroad to extract the raw materials necessary for production. This may be due to either a shortage in domestic supply or cheaper sources elsewhere. Multinationals often possess the finance, technology, and expertise required, whereas local companies do not.
- Production efficiency: Imperfections in the international factor markets encourage companies to locate abroad as an avenue for cutting production costs and increasing competitiveness. Arguably, the labor market is the most imperfect of the factor markets, and recently computer software and insurance companies have established bases in India to take advantage of the skilled, but comparatively low cost, labor force.
- Knowledge seeking: Some companies enter foreign markets with the objective of gaining information and experience that is expected to prove useful. Multinational companies may locate their operations to a place where a high concentration of research and development and expertise exists, for example, Silicon Valley. In industries characterized by rapid innovation and technical developments by foreign competitors, it becomes imperative to monitor developments. Japanese companies have established a reputation for "tearing down" a new foreign product, analyzing how it functions, and then attempting to develop a superior product.
- Political security: The motivation here is to avoid government interference in business activity. This has long been obvious to multinationals involved in industries such as weapon systems, telecommunications, and even computers but can be a factor for other industries. The early 1980s, for example, witnessed a period of heavy European investment in the United States as companies feared a swing toward socialism and more government interference

as a result of the recession at that time. A popular strategy is that of multiple sourcing, whereby companies locate in several locations and produce similar products in each. Although this erodes potential economics of scale, companies have more power in dealing with governments or unions through the possibility of moving production elsewhere.

2. *Economic motives.* Economic motives for FDI relate primarily to imperfections in the markets for products, production factors, and financial assets. Five main areas of competitive advantage are identified by the following:

- Economies of scale: Multinational companies enjoy superiority in economies of scale, managerial expertise, technology, differentiating products, and financial strength. The existence of product and factor market imperfections provides an opportunity for multinational companies to outcompete domestic companies, particularly in industries characterized by worldwide oligopolistic competition.

- Defensive investments: Companies may be motivated to invest abroad to defend both domestic and foreign markets from foreign competition.

- Product theory suggests that new products are initially introduced into domestic markets and then subsequently exported. Following product maturity, the domestic market is threatened by foreign competition. Part of the production process may then be relocated abroad to take advantage of lower costs of factors of production.

- Other motivations for FDI may include the behavior of competitors, a "grow to survive" philosophy, and in the case of service industries, a need to follow the customer.

- The theory of internationalization suggests that companies generating valuable proprietary information can only reap the full benefits by FDI.

3. *Behavioral motives.* Included within the behavioral motives category are the following:

- Receiving a proposal from a foreign government
- Fear of losing a market

- The "bandwagon effect": Apparent success of competitor investing abroad
- Intense competition from abroad in the domestic market

Additional Risks

In addition to the normal risks inherent in any capital investment project, there are additional risk factors to consider when considering investing in the global markets:

1. *Exchange rate risk*. Fluctuating exchange rates can both distort the project cash flows and the desirability of the project. Attempts can be made to estimate future exchange rates using the interest rate and purchasing power parity (PPP) theories, but a comprehensive sensitivity analysis would also be advisable.

2. *Inflation risk*. Emerging countries often tend to be prone to higher inflation rates at both the general and specific price level. As with exchange rates, an inflation factor should be incorporated into the project analysis. The rate of inflation will also often impact the exchange rate of the foreign currency.

3. *Political risk*. Given that the objectives of the multinational company and the government of the host country are likely to differ, some degree of political risk is almost inevitable. Political problems can arise from either government interference or unexpected events that occur in the host country and directly impact the foreign investor. The former is likely to take the form of exchange controls, import restriction, or limits on the repatriation of profits from the host country, often through a withholding tax. Often of more significance to the foreign investor are events such as war or revolution, which may result in the expropriation of corporate assets. A recent example of such action was the expropriation of the assets of foreign cement companies by the Venezuelan government in 2008 following a decision to nationalize the domestic cement industry.

4. *Remittance risk*. Invariably, as a consequence of host government policies, there may be a significant variation between the cash flows generated by the project and the final amounts remitted to the parent company. Cash flows to the parent company provide the

ultimate basis for dividends and reinvestment, but this violates the principle that financial and operating cash flows should remain separate. In spite of the strong argument in favor of utilizing parent cash flows, empirical evidence tends to reveal an almost equal three way split between multinationals using project cash flows, parent cash flows, and both.

Making the Decision

Clearly, a decision to proceed with FDI not only is of major strategic significance but also will involve a substantial financial commitment. The financial commitment can be broadly separated into three components:

1. An initial set up cost, which is likely to be irrecoverable, to establish a production facility, along with any necessary infrastructural investments that may be necessary in more remote locations
2. A recurring fixed cost that is largely independent of the level of output (e.g., management salaries)
3. Recurrent variable costs of labor, raw materials, and so on

As with domestic capital budgeting decisions, the project should be evaluated on the basis of incremental after-tax cash flows. However, one obvious difference is that the cash flows will be denominated in a foreign currency whose exchange value against the domestic currency may fluctuate significantly over what is likely to be a long time horizon. Consequently, it is advisable to attempt to predict potential future exchange rates during the life of the project. The theoretical equilibrium framework for international finance suggests some approximate relationships between exchange rate movements and interest rates or rates of inflation in the domestic and foreign economies. Perhaps the most notable is that of interest rate parity, which suggests that, over time, exchange rates will be largely determined by differences in interest rates between the respective economies.

The basic premise of interest rate parity is that an equilibrium relationship will exist between spot and forward exchange rates and differences in interest rates as follows:

$$(1 + i_\$) = (F/S)(1 + i_£) \text{ or approximately as } (i_\$ - i_£) = (F - S)/S,$$

where

- $i_\$$ and $i_£$ are the respective interest rates in the United States and United Kingdom.
- F and S are the forward and spot rates for the dollar against the pound.

Interest rate parity suggests that the potential interest gain from investing in the economy with the higher interest rate will be exactly cancelled out by a reduction in the value of the currency of that economy; that is, arbitrage will ensure that gains cannot be made by switching into a different currency to take advantage of a higher interest rate and then reverse the transaction.

A similar approach can be undertaken using purchasing power parity, which uses rates of inflation as opposed to interest rates, but the calculations are similar in that the currency in the country with lower inflation will appreciate against the currency with the higher rate of inflation. The relative version of PPP that considers percentage changes in the exchange rate can be estimated from the following simplified equation:

$$\frac{Ert - Ero}{Ero} = \frac{if,t - id,t}{1 + id,t}$$

Ert, Ero are the home currency values of one unit of the foreign currency at times *t* and 0; *if,t* and *id,t* are the expected rates of inflation in the foreign and domestic economies.

Example 9.1

If U.S. interest rates were 2% per annum and UK interest rates were 5% per annum, then the UK pound would be expected to depreciate against the U.S. dollar by approximately 3% per annum due to the interest rate differential. Assuming that the current spot rate was £1 = $1.50, the predicted future rates for the next 5 years are shown in Table 9.1.

A further complicating factor inherent when considering FDI is that of estimating the after-tax cash flows. With domestic investments, there

Table 9.1. Predicted Exchange Rates Using Interest Rate Parity

Year	Rate
1	1.455
2	1.411
3	1.369
4	1.328
5	1.288

is a single corporation tax rate to consider, but with foreign investments, there are likely to be different tax rates in the two countries involved and often a double taxation agreement may be in place (e.g., a double taxation convention was signed between the United Kingdom and the United States on July 24, 2001). In addition, the host government may impose a withholding tax in an attempt to limit repatriation of profits by the multinational company.

In relation to double taxation agreements, generally the multinational is subject to taxation at the higher rate of the two countries involved.

Example 9.2

If the tax rate in country A is 40% and it is 35% in country B, then a company domiciled in country B will pay 40% on profits earned in country A and will not be liable for any additional taxation in its own country (but will also not be entitled to any refund). In contrast, a company domiciled in country A will pay 35% on profits earned in country B and will then be subject to additional taxation of 5% in its own country. The overall taxation charge can also be affected by the amounts of any deductions against income that are applicable.

A third issue is whether the presence of additional economic and political risk unique to foreign investments should be accounted for in either cash flow or discount rate adjustments. Arguably, it is more appropriate to adjust cash flows, since there is normally better information regarding the specific impact of a given risk on a project's cash flow than on its required return.

The suggested evaluation procedure is as follows:

1. Estimate the incremental cash flows in the foreign country, accounting for any foreign tax implications (corporation and withholding taxes).
2. Calculate the cash flows remittable to the parent company and convert these cash flows into the domestic currency using future expected exchange rates for the relevant periods.
3. Adjust the remitted cash flows for any indirect costs or benefits directly caused by implementing the project. Any additional domestic tax effects should be considered during this stage.
4. Discount the parent company's incremental cash flows at a rate that is appropriate for the risk of the project to estimate the expected net present value (NPV) for the project.

Example 9.3

Hedgelea Ltd. is a U.S. company whose domestic market has reached saturation point, and consequently, the board of directors is considering establishing a production facility in a foreign market. After initial screening, two potential investments, which are mutually exclusive due to a limitation on finance available, are being considered.

The first project is an investment in Steadyland, which is regarded as a safe investment in terms of political risk. The second project is in Worryland, which has a history of political unrest and changes in government. Both projects are expected to have a duration of 5 years, though an election is likely in Worryland in 3 years time, and there is a 50% chance of a change of government. This is likely to result in the nationalization of the industry in which Hedgelea operates, and compensation equal to 50% of the value of the initial investment will be paid to Hedgelea.

The current exchange rates between dollars and the foreign currencies (the Steady and the Worry) are as follows:

$$\$1 = 3 \text{ Steadys and } \$1 = 5 \text{ Worrys.}$$

Hedgelea has enlisted the services of an economic forecasting agency, which has provided estimates of expected future rates of inflation in the United States, Steadyland, and Worryland as shown in Table 9.2.

The initial costs of the investments and the expected annual cash inflows (in the foreign currencies) are displayed in Table 9.3. Neither

Table 9.2. Expected Future Rates of Inflation

Year	United States (%)	Steadyland (%)	Worryland (%)
1	3	3	5
2	4	2	8
3	4	2	10
4	5	2	10
5	6	1	6

Table 9.3. Project Costs and Expected Cash Inflows

Project	Cost	Year 1	Year 2	Year 3	Year 4	Year 5
Steady	(60 million)	15 million	25 million	30 million	40 million	50 million
Worry	(60 million)	20 million	40 million	80 million	50 million	60 million

investment is expected to have any residual value at the end of the 5-year period.

As an incentive, the government of Worryland will allow a tax holiday for the first 3 years of the project, and thereafter charge a corporation tax rate of 10%. However, Worryland does not have a tax treaty with the United States, and the U.S. government will charge a tax rate of 30% on profit earned from a foreign subsidiary.

The standard rate of corporation tax in Steadyland is 20% and the country does have a tax treaty with the United States whereby tax paid in Steadyland is offset against that due in the United States. All three tax regimes require payment of taxation to be made in the same year as profits are earned.

Hedgelea has established a discount rate of 15% for foreign investment, but due to the increased political risk in Worryland, it has decided to use a rate of 20% for that country.

Solution

Initially we use PPP to estimate the percentage changes and expected future exchange rates as shown in Table 9.4.

Table 9.4. Estimation of Future Exchange Rates

Spot rate	Steadyland % change	$1 = 3	Worryland % change	$1 = 5
Year 1	0	$1 = 3	0.0194	$1 = 5.097
Year 2	–0.0192	$1 = 2.942	0.0385	$1 = 5.293
Year 3	–0.0192	$1 = 2.889	0.0577	$1 = 5.599
Year 4	–0.0286	$1 = 2.806	0.0476	$1 = 5.865
Year 5	–0.0472	$1= 2.674	0	$1 = 5.865

1. Estimate the incremental cash flows in the foreign countries (see tables 9.5 and 9.6). If there is a change of government in Worryland and nationalization takes place, then the adjusted cash flows will be changed to the numbers in table 9.7.
2. Convert remitted cash flows to domestic currency (see tables 9.8–9.10).
3. Adjust the remitted cash flows for any indirect costs or benefits directly caused by implementing the project and any additional domestic tax effects (see tables 9.11 and 9.12).
4. Discount the parent company incremental cash flows at a rate that is appropriate for the risk of the project (see tables 9.13–9.15).

The expected NPV (ENPV) from the Worryland project is therefore

ENPV = $5.286 million(0.5) + $3.745 million(0.5) = +$4.516 million.

On the basis of NPV, there is little to choose between the projects as they have similar values, though the Steadyland project generates a

Table 9.5. Steadyland

Project	Cost	Year 1	Year 2	Year 3	Year 4	Year 5
Cash flow	(60 million)	15 million	25 million	30 million	40 million	50 million
Taxation (20%)		(3 million)	(5 million)	(6 million)	(8 million)	(10 million)
Net cash flow	(60 million)	12 million	20 million	24 million	32 million	40 million

Table 9.6. Worryland

Project	Cost	Year 1	Year 2	Year 3	Year 4	Year 5
Cash flow	(60 million)	20 million	40 million	80 million	60 million	50 million
Taxation (10%)					(6 million)	(5 million)
Net cash flow	(60 million)	20 million	40 million	80 million	54 million	45 million

Table 9.7. Incremental Cash Flows

Project	Cost	Year 1	Year 2	Year 3	Year 4	Year 5
Cash flow	(60 million)	20 million	40 million	80 million		
Taxation (20%)						
Net cash flow	(60 million)	20 million	40 million	110 million*		

Table 9.8. Steadyland

Project	Cost	Year 1	Year 2	Year 3	Year 4	Year 5
Steady	(60 million)	12 million	20 million	24 million	32 million	40 million
Exchange rate	3	3	2.942	2.889	2.806	2.674
Cash flow($)	(20 million)	4 million	6.8 million	8.31 million	11.4 million	15.0 million

Table 9.9. Worryland Scenario 1: No Nationalization

Project	Cost	Year 1	Year 2	Year 3	Year 4	Year 5
Worry	(60 million)	20 million	40 million	80 million	54 million	45 million
Exchange rate	5	5.097	5.293	5.599	5.865	5.865
Cash flow ($)	(12 million)	3.924 million	7.557 million	14.288 million	9.212 million	7.673 million

Table 9.10. Worryland Scenario 2: Nationalization

Project	Cost	Year 1	Year 2	Year 3	Year 4	Year 5
Worry	(60 million)	20 million	40 million	110 million		
Exchange rate	5	5.097	5.293	5.599		
Cash flow ($)	(12 million)	3.924 million	7.557 million	19.646 million		

Table 9.11. Steadyland

	Year 1 ($)	Year 2 ($)	Year 3 ($)	Year 4 ($)	Year 5 ($)
Taxable revenue	5 million	8.498 million	10.384 million	14.255 million	18.699 million
U.S. tax (30%)	(1.5 million)	(2.549 million)	(3.115 million)	(4.277 million)	(5.610 million)
Tax paid	(1.0 million)	(1.700 million)	(2.077 million)	(2.851 million)	(3.740 million)
Additional tax	(0.5 million)	(0.849 million)	(1.038 million)	(1.426 million)	(1.87 million)

Table 9.12. Worryland (Scenario 1)

	Year 1 ($)	Year 2 ($)	Year 3 ($)	Year 4 ($)	Year 5 ($)
Taxable revenue	4 million	7.848 million	15.114 million	10.230 million	8.525 million
U.S. tax (30%)	(1.2 million)	(2.354 million)	(4.534 million)	(3.069 million)	(2.558 million)
Tax paid				(1.023 million)	(0.853 million)
Total tax	(1.2 million)	(2.354 million)	(4.534 million)	(4.092 million)	(3.411 million)

Table 9.13. Steadyland

Project	Cost	Year 1	Year 2	Year 3	Year 4	Year 5
Cash flow	(20 million)	5 million	8.498 million	10.384 million	14.255 million	18.699 million
Total tax		(1.5 million)	(2.549 million)	(3.115 million)	(4.277 million)	(5.610 million)
Net	(20 million)	3.5 million	5.949 million	7.269 million	9.978 million	13.089 million
15% discount	1.000	0.870	0.756	0.658	0.572	0.497
P value	(20 million)	3.045 million	4.497 million	4.783 million	5.707 million	6.505 million

NPV = + $4.537 million

Table 9.14. Worryland: Scenario 1

Project	Cost	Year 1	Year 2	Year 3	Year 4	Year 5
Cash flow	(12 million)	4 million	7.848 million	15.114 million	10.230 million	8.525 million
Total tax		(1.2 million)	(2.354 million)	(4.534 million)	(4.092 million)	(3.411 million)
Net	(12 million)	2.8 million	5.494 million	10.58 million	6.138 million	5.114 million
20% discount	1.000	0.833	0.694	0.579	0.482	0.402
P value	(12 million)	2.332 million	3.813 million	6.126 million	2.959 million	2.056 million

NPV = + $5.286 million

Table 9.15. Worryland: Scenario 2

Project	Cost	Year 1	Year 2	Year 3
Cash flow	(12 million)	4 million	7.848 million	15.114 million
Total tax		(1.2 million)	(2.354 million)	(4.534 million)
Net	(12 million)	2.8 million	5.494 million	10.58 million
Compensation				6.00 million
20% discount	1.000	0.833	0.694	0.579
P value	(12 million)	2.332 million	3.813 million	9.600 million

NPV = + $3.745 million

slightly higher value. However, there is a 50% probability that the Worryland project generates a higher NPV and a similar probability that the NPV is lower. The final decision may be made primarily on the basis of the firm's attitude toward risk, with the Steadyland project being the safer option.

This example is relatively straightforward and excludes other potential complications, such as withholding taxes and management fees, which are often present in such decisions. The amount of risk involved with FDI is clearly significantly higher than domestic investments due particularly to foreign currency and political risks. It would be advisable to perform a sensitivity or scenario analysis using differing assumptions regarding exchange rates and probabilities of adverse events, such as the expropriation of assets. Services are available that provide a ranking of countries based on their political risk, which is usually a composite of various sub-risks that include economic risks and so on. It is also possible for firms to insure themselves against the possible expropriation of assets using schemes that are available through domestic governments.

Survey Evidence

Perhaps the primary research question regarding FDI decisions is whether firms use different techniques when compared to domestic investments. A further question concerns the perception of risk, as it is reasonable to argue that overall corporate risk may either increase or decrease as a result of FDI, depending on the view taken. As we have discussed, FDI involves additional risks when compared to domestic projects and therefore appears inherently more risky, but, despite this, overall corporate risk may be regarded as decreasing on the basis of diversification benefits.

The most comprehensive empirical study analyzing international investment decision was performed in the United States[2] and surveyed 483 of the largest U.S. companies identified as multinationals on the basis of operating in at least six foreign countries. Responses were received from 146 companies regarding the perceived risk of FDI and the cost of capital used in the appraisal process. With respect to overall risk, the majority of companies (68.7%) believed that FDI increased their risk exposure versus the 31.3% that indicated that risk exposure was reduced. The most significant types of risk were deemed to be economic risk (38%), currency risk (27.2%), and expropriation risk (20.5%) with those selecting expropriation concentrated mainly in the extractive industries and having their largest investment in Latin America. The predominant method of measuring risk was a subjective approach, based on top management perceptions (76%) as opposed to an objective measure.

Multinationals must also decide whether to use either the parent firm's cost of capital or the subsidiary's when evaluating a project. The normative recommendation is that the corporate-wide weighted average cost of capital should be used, which could be adjusted for the risk of a particular country or project. Respondents indicated that just over half (53.8%) used the corporate-wide rate. Another key factor in the investment decision concerns the method used for evaluating the profits and cash flow from the investment. Again, the normative recommendation would be that the relevant measure should be the amount of cash flow contributed to the parent company. However, the survey revealed only 39.3% stated that they used remittance to the parent, with the majority of 60.7% using the subsidiary's profit or cash flow. A possible explanation is the desire of management to be evaluated on the basis of performance on a local basis rather than on remittances to the parent company.

A more recent survey in Sweden[3] examined the capital budgeting techniques used for FDI and, in particular, investigated whether the choice of method was influenced by the degree of political risk involved. A total of 497 Swedish companies were surveyed, from which 145 usable responses were received, with the average firm having FDIs in eight countries representing 25% of assets. The results can be summarized as follows:

1. All four main techniques (NPV, internal rate of return [IRR], payback, accounting rate of return [ARR]) were employed by a majority of firms with payback proving the most popular at 79%, followed by NPV at 69%, ARR at 65%, and IRR at 62%. Of particular interest was the finding that 40% of the firms used payback more often than NPV for FDI investments (32% equally often and 28% less often).

2. When dealing with investments involving perceived higher levels of political risk, 43% of the respondents indicated a change in decision criteria. In addition to using higher hurdle rates, shorter payback periods, or both, it was noted that the frequency with which NPV is used declines with increasing risk of expropriation. A possible

explanation was that managers find difficulty in taking such risks into account and rely on simple rules of thumb (use of payback increases with risk of expropriation).

A final point made in this study was that political risk may be socially costly in the sense that there is likely to be a bias in favor of short-term investments, which potentially reduce the benefits for the host country in addition to reducing the level of foreign investment.

CHAPTER 10

Recent Developments

Arguably, the most significant theoretical development in capital budgeting in recent times has been the attempt to apply the option valuation models originally associated with financial options to investment projects via the concept of "real options," which essentially introduce learning and flexibility as a source of value. A significant portion of this chapter will be devoted to explaining the potential application of real options theory to specific types of decisions and exploring alternative methods for estimating the value of such options. In addition, other recent innovations emerging from the capital budgeting literature, which include, inter alia, duration analysis, cash flow value at risk, and decision markets, will be identified and their potential evaluated.

Why Real Options?

Contemporary corporate project appraisal techniques treat capital projects as if they are financial instruments, such as shares or bonds. Indeed, net present value (NPV) was initially developed to value one-off, passive investment strategies, such as whether to invest in bonds, but was subsequently applied to project valuation. Consequently, NPV is a one-off decision implying that investment plans are not modified, regardless of how conditions change. In reality, managers can observe the accuracy of their forecasts along with competitor reactions and market characteristics. If necessary, they can make a strategic decision to increase or decrease the size of the investment, or even abandon if appropriate (i.e., real options). Conventional discounted cash flow analysis does not lend itself to estimating the correct value of flexible projects, because it does not provide the methodology for measuring the value of real options that offer flexibility. According to Dixit and Pindyck, "The net present value rule is not sufficient. To make intelligent choices, managers need to consider the value of keeping their options open."[1]

It is in terms of strategic application that the real power of real options resides. It has been further suggested[2] that the "use of options methodology gives managers a better handle on uncertainty." The process of attempting to identify and subsequently value real options encourages managers to search for value creating opportunities. In identifying options, strategies are discovered because strategies are defined by the decisions taken. Indeed, it has been suggested that strategic management is similar to a series of options[3] and even that all business decisions are real options in conferring the right, but not the obligation, to take some initiative in the future.[4]

Similarities Between Financial and Real Options

The Black-Scholes option valuation model suggests that the value of a financial option depends on five factors: the current share price (S), the strike price of the option (K), the risk-free interest rate (R), the time to maturity (τ), and volatility (σ). The value of a call option is increased by all the factors except the strike price. The same model can be utilized to value a real option with comparable variables relating to the project under consideration by replacing those variables relevant to the financial option (see Table 10.1).

Of particular note is that the value of a real option increases with volatility (i.e., uncertainty regarding the cash flows). This would appear to contrast with the normal approach to project appraisal, where adjustments for uncertainty (risk-adjusted discount rates, etc.) would tend to decrease the attractiveness of the project. The difference with real options

Table 10.1. Comparison of Financial and Real Option Variables

Variable	Financial option	Real option
S	Current share price	Present Value of expected cash flows
K	Strike price	Cost of investment
R	Risk-free interest rate	Risk-free interest rate
σ	Share price volatility	Cash flow volatility
τ	Time to maturity	Time until opportunity expires

is that there is no obligation to exercise the option unless the expected value is positive. This has the effect of limiting the downside of real options to the investment cost, thereby truncating the probability distribution of the payoffs.

Taking into account the importance of including strategic possibilities, a modified version of NPV for investment decisions was proposed.[5] This included the value of the option in the criterion for acceptance:

accept when conventional NPV + option value > 0

Clearly, this rule is likely to be of most significance when the project is marginal in terms of NPV. If the NPV of the investment is very highly positive (or negative), it will be accepted (or rejected) anyway, so the added complexity of valuing the option is not really warranted. In other words, real options are similar to financial options in that their value is highest when the option is "at the money."

Valuation Techniques

The valuation of real options poses more difficulties than that of financial options. The two main valuation techniques are the continuous time framework of the Black-Scholes model and the discrete time framework of the binomial option pricing model. Of the two, it could be argued that the latter is commonly more flexible and intuitively appealing. We shall illustrate each method by means of an example and also discuss their inherent problems.

Black-Scholes Model

For sake of simplicity we shall utilize the non-dividend-paying version of the Black-Scholes model:

$$\text{option value} = SN(d1) - Ke^{-rt}N(d2),$$

where

$$d1 = \frac{Ln\ (S/K) + (R + 0.5\sigma 2)\ \tau}{\sigma\sqrt{\tau}}$$

$$d2 = d1 - \sigma\sqrt{\tau}$$

Example 10.1

PB Oil Plc has the opportunity to acquire a 5-year license on an unexplored oil field. When developed, the block is expected to yield 50 million barrels of oil. The current price of a barrel of oil is $10, and the present value of the costs of developing the field is $600 million.

Advise the company as to whether the license should be acquired using the following:

1. NPV
2. Real options approach

The NPV of the opportunity is given by

$$NPV = \$500 \text{ million} - \$600 \text{ million} = -\$100 \text{ million},$$

and on this basis, the company would clearly reject the opportunity.

To apply the Black-Scholes option valuation formula, we require some further information. The sources of uncertainty that the company faces relate to the quantity and price of oil and we shall assume that together they result in a 30% standard deviation for the value of the operating cash flow. The license expires in 5 years' time and we shall assume a risk-free interest rate of 5% per annum:

$$\text{option value} = 500 \ N(d1) - 600e^{-0.25}N(d2),$$

where

$$d1 = \frac{Ln \ (500/600) + (0.05 + 0.5(0.3)2) \ 5}{0.3\sqrt{5}} = 0.437$$

$$d2 = 0.437 - 0.3\sqrt{5} = -0.234$$

From normal distribution tables,

$$N(0.437) = 0.67 \text{ and } N(-0.234) = 0.41,$$

therefore,

$$\text{option value} = 500(0.67) - 600e^{-0.25}(0.41) = \$143.4 \text{ million.}$$

The difference between this result and the result achieved using NPV, in this case $243.4 million, represents the value of the flexibility inherent in not having to decide on the full investment immediately but being able to wait and decide when the uncertainty is resolved.

As previously mentioned, increasing the uncertainty increases the value of the option. If, for example, we increase the level of uncertainty regarding the quantity and price to 40%, then the value of the option would be

$$\text{option value} = 500(0.70) - 600e^{-0.25}(0.36) = \$181.7 \text{ million.}$$

One of the advantages of using the modified Black-Scholes approach to value real options is that the variables influencing the value of the option can be further investigated. In particular, the sensitivity of the option value to changes in the variables can be evaluated (see Table 10.2).

Clearly, in this example, the value of the option is particularly sensitive to the value of the oil and relatively insensitive to changes in the risk-free rate of interest.

Using the Black-Scholes model for valuing real options implicitly makes the standard replicating portfolio assumption of financial option pricing; that is, that a portfolio of traded investments can be constructed to replicate the returns of the option in question. As a result, the option can be valued based on the standard no-arbitrage argument, which implies that the value of the option does not depend on investors' risk preferences.

In practice, most real options, apart from commodity based projects, cannot be hedged, since there is little reason to expect that a specific manufacturing or R and D project would be highly correlated with a particular stock. Consequently, this identifies the inherent weakness in using the Black-Scholes method.

Table 10.2. Sensitivity of Option Values to 10% Change

Variable	Current value	+10%	Option value	Change (%)
S	500	550	204.3	+ 42.5
K	600	660	125.0	−12.8
R	0.05	0.055	144.5	+0.8
σ	30%	33%	157.7	+10
τ	5 years	5.5 years	153	+6.7

Binomial Option Pricing Model (BOPM)

Intermediate cash flows cause difficulties for option valuation in both real and financial options. For example, dividend payments can be incorporated into the Black-Scholes model, but it relies on the assumption that the payments constitute a continuous cash flow. In reality, cash flows are more likely to be discrete, and the BOPM lends itself more readily to this scenario. In addition, it permits early exercise (American option) to be modeled, which is a feature of most real options. From a practical viewpoint, it also produces a better picture of how underlying cash flows and the corresponding option values evolve. We shall initially consider a simple one period binomial model in example 10.2.

Example 10.2

BOP Plc is considering a project that currently has a present value of $10 million but costs $12 million. At the end of 1 year, the present value will either increase to $15 million or decrease to $5 million with equal probability.

Estimate the value of the project using the following:

1. NPV
2. An option to wait for 1 year

The risk-free rate of interest is 5%. Clearly, the project is unacceptable as a one-off decision, with an NPV of –$2 million. The future present values are expressed as a binomial tree in Figure 10.1.

In this case, the present value can either increase by 50% ($u = 1.5$) or decrease by 50% ($d = 0.5$). The binomial model then proceeds by calculating the risk-neutral probabilities (q and $1 - q$) as follows:

$$q = \frac{e^r - d}{u - d} = \frac{e^{0.05} - 0.5}{1.5 - 0.5} = 0.55$$

$$1 - q = 1 - 0.55 = 0.45$$

Since the option to defer the project for 1 year gives the managers the right, but not the obligation, to make the investment by next year, they

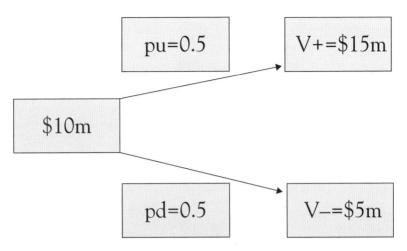

Figure 10.1. Binomial tree representation of project.

will wait and proceed with the investment if its value next year exceeds the investment at that time. In other words, the option to defer is essentially a call option on the project's value, V, with an exercise price equal to the required outlay a year later. The binomial lattice is then shown in Figure 10.2.

The value of the option when the present value increases, $C+$, is obtained by assuming that the required investment increases by the risk-free rate if delayed for 1 year. That is,

$$C+ = \$15 \text{ million} - (\$12 \text{ million} \times 1.05) = \$2.4 \text{ million.}$$

The present value of the option, Co, is obtained from

$$Co = \frac{q\ C+ + (1 - q)\ C-}{1 + r} = \frac{0.55(2.4) + 0.45(0)}{1.05} = \$1.257 \text{ million.}$$

Compared to evaluating the project using NPV, the value of the option is

$$\text{value of option} = \$1.257 \text{ million} - (-\$2 \text{ million}) = \$3.257 \text{ million,}$$

which equates to 27% of the original investment.

The one-period binomial model provides a good starting point for the analysis of real options but the typical real option will usually be more

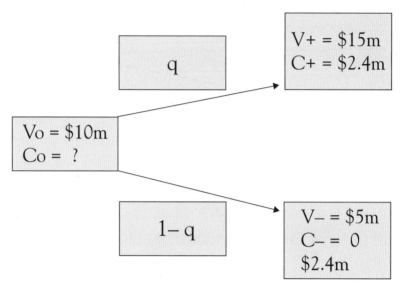

Figure 10.2. Binomial lattice for deferment option.

complex than it is possible to represent by the one-period model. To get closer to reality requires us to extend the model to a multiperiod context.

An Alternative Approach

Some of the mathematical complexities of the Black-Scholes and binomial models can be avoided in an alternative approach to the valuation of real options.[6] This approach claims that two types of uncertainty affect real investment: uncertainty concerning the present value that the investment may generate and uncertainty about the investment required. These two variables are then combined into the profitability index (PI), and the problem focuses on the distribution of potential values of the investment's PI. The real option will only then be exercised if the value of the PI equals or exceeds unity.

The rejection of PIs less than one clearly alters the distribution of the PIs and, in turn, the risk. A risk-neutral approach is again necessary, but this is achieved by calculation of a risk-adjustment factor given by

$$F = \frac{\text{risk adjustment factor for present value } (PV)}{\text{risk adjustment factor for investment } (I),}$$

where

$$\text{risk adjustment factor for } (PV) = \frac{(1 + Rf)^T}{(1 + RPV)^T}$$

and

$$\text{risk adjustment factor for } (I) = \frac{(1 + Rf)^T}{(1 + RI)^T},$$

where RPV is the project's discount rate, RI the discount rate for future investment expenditure, and T the time prior to exercising the option.

$$F = \frac{(1 + Rf)^T}{(1 + RPV)^T} \times \frac{(1 + RI)^T}{(1 + Rf)^T} = \frac{(1 + RI)^T}{(1 + RPV)^T}$$

Since the project discount rate will generally exceed the discount rate for the future investment expenditure, the value of F will be less than unity.

The risk adjustment factor (F) is then applied to the distribution of the PIs, which has the effect of reducing their values and hence the overall expected PI of the project. However, the smaller expected payoff does not require any further discounting.

Example 10.3

Bramble Plc is a pharmaceutical company considering spending $8 million on research and development over the next 4 years prior to undertaking a project that will require a further outlay of $30 million.

The expected PI of the project is calculated in Table 10.3 from information regarding the distribution of potential PIs.

Table 10.3. Distribution of Potential PIs

Interval	Midvalue	Probability	PI of payoff	Expected PI
$0 < x \le 0.5$	0.25	0.11	1.00	0.110
$0.5 < x \le 1.0$	0.75	0.22	1.00	0.220
$1.0 < x \le 1.5$	1.25	0.34	1.25	0.425
$1.5 < x \le 2.0$	1.75	0.22	1.75	0.385
$2.0 < x \le 2.5$	2.25	0.11	2.25	0.248
			PI =	1.388

In the first two rows, the management do not invest in the project since PI < 1. So instead, the funds are invested in the financial market, where, by definition, the PI = 1. The expected value of the PI (1.388) occurs 4 years in the future and therefore requires discounting. We shall assume that RI is 6% and RPV is 10%, thereby yielding the following risk-adjustment factor:

$$F = \frac{(1 + 0.06)^4}{(1 + 0.10)^4} = 0.86$$

This factor is then applied to the original distribution of PIs to yield the results found in Table 10.4.

$$\text{PV of option} = \frac{30}{1.064} \times 0.273 = \$6.487 \text{ million}$$

The present value of the option can then be obtained by multiplying the investment required in year 4 by the net profitability index and then discounting back to the present.

Therefore, the research and development expenditure required to avail of the option in 4 years' time is $2 million a year for 4 years. In present value terms, this is valued at

PV of R and D = $2 million × 3.465 = $6.93 million.

Table 10.4. Application of Risk-Adjustment Factor

Interval	Midvalue	Probability	PI of payoff	Expected PI
0 < x ≤ 0.43	0.215	0.11	1.00	0.110
0.43 < x ≤ 0.86	0.645	0.22	1.00	0.220
0.86 < x ≤ 1.29	1.075	0.34	1.172*	0.399
1.29 < x ≤ 1.72	1.505	0.22	1.505	0.331
1.72 < x ≤ 2.15	1.935	0.11	1.935	0.213
			PI =	1.273

*1 × (013/0.43) + 1.29 × (0.29/0.43) = 1.172

In this case, the present value of the required R and D expenditure exceeds the present value of the option by $443,000 and, on the basis of these assumptions, would not be undertaken.

Applications of Real Options

A classification of real options according to type has been proposed as follows:[7]

- *Timing options.* Options to embark on a project, to defer it, or to abandon it
- *Scale options.* Options to expand or contract an investment
- *Staging options.* Options to undertake an investment in stages
- *Growth options.* Options to make small investments that may lead to greater opportunities
- *Switching options.* Options to switch the inputs or outputs in a production process

Timing Options

The option to defer investment in a project will increase shareholder value if the present value of the option to invest at a later date exceeds that from investing immediately. The value of the option will be determined primarily by the intensity of competition and the potential impact of new information becoming available during the delay. Recent literature has investigated the significance of "first mover advantage" in specific market structures.[8] Furthermore, there may be an opportunity cost emanating from lost income during the period of delay.

If a project does not live up to expectations, then it may be preferable to reduce planned expenditure or even abandon the project. Management may decide to create a strategic abandonment option within a specified period of time if the project is not deemed successful. For example, the development of a drug in the pharmaceutical industry may take several years and go through various phases of testing and regulatory approval. In event of abandonment, it may be possible to sell the intellectual property rights of the drug to another pharmaceutical company by means of a contractual agreement. Alternatively, in the case of an investment in capital equipment, it may be possible to sell the equipment in the event of an abandonment decision. In the latter case, the value of the option may be relatively small depending on the specificity of the equipment to the industry in question.

Scale Options

Beginning with an initial level of capacity, there is often the opportunity to expand (a call option) or contract (a put option) from that level. If market conditions turn out more favorable than projected, management can accelerate the rate or expand the scale of production. A more expensive technology may be chosen initially for built-in flexibility to expand production if and when it becomes desirable. If market conditions turn out to be less favorable than predicted, management can operate below capacity or even reduce the scale of operations, thereby cutting back on planned investment. This disinvestment may produce a cash inflow from the sale of redundant assets or require an exit cost to be paid from reducing employment. Both types of options may be particularly valuable following new product launches in uncertain markets.

Staging Options

In most real-life projects, the required expenditure is not incurred as a single up-front outlay but rather as a series of outlays over time. This staging or phasing of expenditure creates valuable options to "default" at any given time. Consequently, each stage can be viewed as an option on the value of subsequent stages by incurring the outlay required to proceed to the next stage. It is therefore important that the progress of the project, and the available options, are thoroughly reviewed at each stage. Projects with long development periods will typically be subject to more uncertainty and should be managed so that there is greater flexibility to compensate.

Such options are also valuable in R and D-intensive industries, such as pharmaceuticals and in venture-capital financing, where there are options to sell or float the company being financed as a means of recovering the investment.

Growth Options

Corporate growth options that shape the path for future opportunities are clearly of considerable strategic importance. Many early investments (e.g., R and D, an IT network, strategic acquisition, expansion overseas) can be viewed as prerequisites or links in a chain of interrelated projects. The value of such projects often arises not so much from expected cash flows but rather from the future growth opportunities that may be unlocked (new technology, strategic positioning, access to a new market). An entry into initially loss-making business operations may make way for potentially valuable follow-on opportunities. Such was the case with many Internet ventures, which strived to establish a critical mass of customers. However, unless the initial investment is made, subsequent investments or applications will not be feasible. Options for growth are found in all infrastructure-based or strategic industries. The valuation of such compound options is often difficult to estimate, but such options are often the most valuable. Some caution may be necessary in estimating the potential value of future opportunities, as was evident in the case of telecom companies paying for third generation (3G) licenses.

Switching Options

The flexibility to switch from the current input to the cheapest future input, or to switch from the current output to the most profitable future output, may prove valuable as the relative prices of the inputs or outputs fluctuate over time. For example, a generating station could be powered by a variety of fuels, such as oil, gas, or coal. A generating station that is capable of switching from one fuel to another will have an advantage over a similar station without that capability. However, the construction costs of the former station are likely to be higher (i.e., flexibility comes at a price). The issue then becomes one of valuing the flexibility to switch inputs against the extra costs. Similarly, a multinational company may locate production facilities in different locations to acquire the flexibility to shift production as relative costs or exchange rates fluctuate over time.

The flexibility to switch outputs, product flexibility, is valuable in industries such as automobiles, consumer electronics, toys, and pharmaceuticals, where product differentiation and diversity are important and product demand is volatile. Again, it may be worthwhile to install a more expensive flexible capacity with the facility to alter product mix or the scale of production in line with changing market trends.

Real Options in Practice

In a highly regarded text published in 2001,[9] the claim was made that real options would dominate the capital budgeting process within the next decade. We conclude this section by assessing the extent to which this prediction has come true by examining both the survey evidence that existed prior to 2001 and that which has subsequently been published.

An empirical study of the views of senior finance managers of the FTSE 100 companies[10] suggested that very few decision makers were aware of the formal academic research in this area. It was generally agreed that flexibility occurred quite frequently and was often necessary for the acceptance of the investment proposal. However, flexibility was not always seen as desirable in developing commitment to the planned program, and may not even be available in the presence of regulatory or commercial commitments. Those decision makers who were aware of the academic research believed that it had to be made much more accessible to managers before it could be widely utilized.

Similarly, a European study[11] reported that respondents possessed a somewhat inadequate knowledge of academic research on real options. Some oil and mineral companies quantified real options and a few companies in high-growth areas qualitatively allowed for their existence.

A more recent study in the United States[12] claimed that companies used real options as a strategic way of thinking, an analytical valuation tool, and a technique for evaluating, monitoring, and managing capital investments. In particular, quantification appeared most prevalently used among oil, energy, and commodity companies.

Further U.S. surveys[13] reported utilization rates of 11.4% and 9%, with real options analysis seemingly viewed as an afterthought and with little analysis or few follow-up questions.

Most recently, a comprehensive questionnaire surveyed the Fortune 1000 companies and received 279 usable responses.[14] Of these, 14.3% indicated some use of real options, with the majority of users represented by the technology and energy industries. The main areas of application reported were new product introduction (36.2%) and research and development (27.8%), with the binomial approach to valuation proving the most popular as only one company reported use of the Black-Scholes model. Those companies not using real options gave four main reasons:

- Lack of top management support (42.7%)
- Discounted cash flow is a proven technique (25.6%)
- Requires too much sophistication (19.5%)
- Encourages too much risk taking (12.2%)

Interestingly, however, 43.5% of those surveyed indicated that they will seriously consider the use of real options in the future, 15.9% suggested there was some possibility of usage, and only 26.3% totally rejected the potential application of real options.

From the survey evidence, it would appear that real options theory remains at the frontier of business knowledge, and the complexities of valuing real options remain too complicated for managers in its current form. Few companies have procedures for either identifying or valuing real options, and procedures that were used generally referred to "risk" rather than "flexibility." Future research should perhaps attempt a case study approach, examining the apparently small number of companies actively incorporating real options into strategic investment decisions in an attempt to make the techniques more accessible to decision makers elsewhere.

Duration Analysis

Although the concept of duration has existed for a significant period of time, it is only relatively recently that its application has extended to capital budgeting. It was originally derived in 1938[15] and for most of the intervening period was applied to bond analysis as a measure of the sensitivity of bond prices to interest rate changes. In essence, it equates to a payback measure for bonds in that it measures how long, in years, it takes for the price of a bond to be repaid from its cash flows (coupon payments and redemption value).

Table 10.5. Calculation of Bond Duration

Time period (T)	Cash flow	Present value	T × present value
1	50	47.62	47.62
2	50	45.35	90.70
3	50	43.19	129.57
4	50	41.14	164.56
5	50	39.18	195.90
5	1,000	783.53	3917.65
		1000	4546.0

Example 10.4

A 5-year bond pays a coupon rate of 5% and has a par value of $1,000. The coupon is paid annually and interest rates are 5%. The duration of the bond can be estimated as shown in Table 10.5.

$$\text{Duration} = 4{,}546/1{,}000 = 4.546 \text{ years}$$

Duration is then used to find an approximate percentage change in the bond price given a change in the discount rate. In the previous example, if the discount rate changed by 0.1%, then the predicted change in the bond price would be

$$\text{change in price} = -4.546 \times (0.1/1.05) = 0.433\%.$$

Consequently, bonds with higher duration will be subject to greater changes in price in the event of interest rates changing.

With capital projects, a sensitivity analysis is a very common exercise when forecasting cash flows. It has been suggested that as an alternative, a duration-type measure could be derived providing a single figure for the assessment of project cash flows relative to change in either the discount rate or a specific cash flow parameter. Recent research has derived the necessary equations and also provided an appendix containing VBA code for Excel-type functions.[16] The use of duration is illustrated in an example where NPV and payback measures are also calculated (see Table 10.6).

The three projects considered in Table 10.6 clearly have almost identical cash flows, with slight variations in the timing of the cash inflows. More specifically, projects B and C have no cash inflows in years 1 and

Table 10.6. Duration Measure for Project Evaluation

Time	Project A cash flows	Project B cash flows	Project C cash flows
0	(1,000)	(1,000)	(1,000)
1	220	0	220
2	242	242	242
3	266.2	266.2	266.2
4	292.82	292.82	292.82
5	322.10	322.10	0
6	354.31	708.62	708.62
NPV*	200	200	200
Payback	3.928 years	4.618 years	3.928 years
Discounted payback	5 years	6 years	6 years
Duration	3.5	4.33	3.67
Effect of 0.1% increase	–0.32%	–0.39%	–0.33%

*A discount rate of 10% has been assumed.

5, respectively, but this is compensated by having a higher cash inflow in year 6 vis-à-vis project A.

On the basis of NPV, we cannot distinguish between the three projects as all predict the same NPV. However, as a consequence of the timing differences, projects B and C are more susceptible to changes in the discount rate as measured by duration than project A. Consequently, if the projects were mutually exclusive or a capital constraint existed, then project A would be preferred to both B and C, and C would be preferred to B. The use of duration is therefore seen as assisting in the decision process when the projects under consideration have either identical or very similar NPVs. Indeed, it could transpire that a project with a marginally lower NPV, but significantly lower duration, may be preferred to a competing project with a marginally higher NPV.

Alternatively, calculation of payback reveals projects A and C to exhibit shorter paybacks than project B, as a consequence of the latter failing to produce any return until the second year. Discounted payback reveals both projects B and C to take longer to recoup the initial investment than project A. Therefore, the payback method, through its emphasis on earlier cash flows, does to some extent capture some of what duration measures because cash flows that accumulate faster result in lower durations. However, the main issue with payback is that postpayback cash flows are not considered.

The impact of a 0.1% increase in the discount rate would appear relatively insignificant in percentage terms, though it should be recognized that the impact of duration is commensurate with the scale of the project. With very large cash flows, even seemingly small differences between project durations may translate into significant amounts.

In the same way as a measure of duration has been estimated for variations in the discount rate, it is also possible to generate comparable duration measures for the parameters that generate the cash flow. The research suggests that the main advantage of duration is that a single figure provides the same intuition as performing a sensitivity analysis, without the associated difficulty of interpreting the results.

Decision Markets

The notion underlying a decision (or alternatively prediction or ideas futures) market is that a marketplace is a better organizer of insight and predictor of the future than individuals. Decision markets originated with the establishment of the Iowa Electronic Markets in 1988 and since then have not only correctly predicted the outcome of every U.S. presidential election but also consistently outpredicted polls and political forecasting experts with an average margin of error of 1.5%.

The use of decision markets expanded during the 1990s[17] to predict a variety of events to include, inter alia, project completion dates, new product sales, and project costs, which are all significant inputs into the capital budgeting process. Essentially, the modus operandi of decision markets is that an internal betting market is set up within the company, and predictions are obtained from managers who wish to profit from their expertise and knowledge about certain events. The market can function using either real cash or virtual cash, which is then used to bet on possible outcomes. The outcome receiving the most cash from the managers is then considered the most likely to occur.

Accurate prediction of the outcome will then generate a return for the successful managers, with most decision markets paying one dollar (or some multiple thereof) for a winning prediction and nothing for a losing prediction. It can be shown that the price of a claim will then approximate the probability of the predictions coming true. Thus, for example, if a claim is priced at 80 cents then there is an 80% probability of that prediction coming true, while a claim priced at 20 cents denotes a 20% probability. A decision guide could then be established on the basis of such probabilities; for example, a probability of 0.75 or above would denote a significant chance of a prediction coming true and a control procedure could be invoked. In contrast, a probability of 0.25 or less would indicate a relatively small chance of a predicted outcome occurring.

Despite the apparent successes of decision markets in diverse predictions such as election outcomes and the box office success of new movies (Hollywood Stock Exchange), relatively few companies have experimented with decision markets. However, there a few notable exceptions:

1. *Google*. Google set up a predictive market system within the company that was designed to forecast product launch dates, new office openings, and a range of other decisions of strategic importance to Google. The Google decision market does not require any payment to play and, to date, more than a thousand Googlers have bid on 146 events in 43 different subject areas. The Google search engine works well because it aggregates information dispersed across the Web, and the internal predictive markets are based on the same principle.

2. *Hewlett Packard (HP)*. HP introduced decision markets in response to ongoing difficulties in estimating printer sales. Initially, a trading platform was set up and a number of employees, mostly product and finance managers, were each given about $50 in a trading account to bet on what they thought computer sales would be at the end of the month. The outcome was that while HP's official forecast, which was generated by a marketing manager, was off by 13%, the decision market was off by only 6%. In further trials, the market beat official forecasts 75% of the time. Intrigued by the success of the trials, HP's business-services division then ran a pilot with 14 managers worldwide, attempting to predict the group's monthly sales and profit. The market was so successful (in one case, improving the prediction by 50%) that it has since been integrated into the division's regular forecasts. Another division is running a pilot to see if a market

would be better at predicting the costs of certain components with volatile prices.

3. *Eli Lilly.* Eli Lilly, one of the largest pharmaceutical companies in the world, ran an experiment in which about 50 employees involved in drug development—chemists, biologists, project managers—traded six mock drug candidates through an internal market. The rationale was to predict which of its new products were likely to make it to the next stage of clinical trials. "We wanted to look at the way scattered bits of information are processed in the course of drug development," says Alpheus Bingham, vice president for Lilly Research Laboratories strategy. Commensurate with the success reported elsewhere, the three drugs identified by the internal decision market as having the highest probability of success were indeed the most successful, while the three with the lowest probabilities turned out to be failures.

Decision markets work because they create incentives for widely dispersed people to reveal information about which they feel confident; gather the knowledge of many diverse and independent minds; decentralize the forecasting process, balancing out mistakes; bypass hierarchical restrictions on knowledge flow; and, finally, aggregate all those opinions efficiently.

Given the universal recognition of the challenges posed by uncertainty for forecasting—and the decisions informed by forecasts—it would seem appropriate for companies to rapidly adopt any method that has proved effective at penetrating the unknown and returned with relatively reliable forecasts. Decision markets (or idea futures markets) are just such a method. However, despite the reported benefits, as of yet, U.S. companies appear to have shown little interest in the technique. As James Suroweicki wrote in *The Wisdom of Crowds*, "the most mystifying thing about decision markets is how little interest corporate America has shown in them."[18]

One likely reason for the lack of adoption of information, prediction, or decision markets is executives' fear that decision markets will take away their ability to set strategy and make choices. Even if that were going to happen, boards of directors should be pushing for these markets anyway. Executives need not worry, however, since they can use decision markets to inform major decisions, rather than to make those decisions for them. Other companies may not have tried this potentially profitable forecasting and decision tool due to lack of knowledge.

In relation to capital budgeting, decision markets can assist companies in predicting not only cash flows from new projects but also the variability of such cash flows and their correlation with existing corporate cash flows. It would appear that the potential of decision markets remains relatively untapped by the majority of companies despite the reported successes.

Cash Flow Value at Risk

Although the concept of value at risk (VAR) has been applied mainly by financial institutions in examining their susceptibility to market risk, there is no reason risk cannot be defined more broadly or narrowly in specific contexts and applied to large investment projects, most probably those of a strategic nature.

The mechanics of VAR, which focused on constructing efficient equity portfolios for investors, were present in portfolio theory from the early 1960s. The emphasis on market risks and the comovement or correlation between such risks is central to the computation of VAR. In contrast to other measures of risk, such as standard deviation, VAR deals primarily with downside risk and downside losses. The computation of VAR depends on three key variables:

1. A specified level of loss of value
2. A fixed time period for assessing the risk
3. A confidence interval

Example 10.5

VAR can be adjusted for different time periods, since some users may be concerned about daily risk whereas others may be more interested in weekly, monthly, or even annual risk. We can rely on the idea that the standard deviation of returns tends to increase with the square root of time to convert from one time period to another. For example, if we wished to convert a daily standard deviation to a monthly equivalent the adjustment would be

$$\sigma_{monthly} = \sigma_{daily} \times \sqrt{T},$$

where T = 20 trading days.

For example, assume that after applying the variance-covariance method we estimate that the daily standard deviation of the FT100 index is 2.5%, and we wish to estimate the maximum loss for 95% and 99% confidence intervals for daily, weekly, and monthly periods assuming 5 trading days each week and 4 trading weeks each month:

95% confidence

daily = $-1.65 \times 2.5\% = -4.125\%$

weekly = $-1.65 \times 2.5\% \times \sqrt{5} = -9.22\%$

monthly = $-1.65 \times 2.5\% \times \sqrt{20} = -18.45\%$

99% confidence

daily = $-2.33 \times 2.5\% = -5.825\%$

weekly = $-2.33 \times 2.5\% \times \sqrt{5} = -13.03\%$

monthly = $-2.33 \times 2.5\% \times \sqrt{20} = -26.05\%$

Therefore, we could say with 95% confidence that we would not lose more than 9.22% per week or with 99% confidence that we would not lose more than 26.05% per month.

The first coining of the term VAR is usually attributed to JP Morgan in 1995, when it made public information on variances and covariance across various security and asset classes. Subsequently, the measure became popular with commercial and investment banks and their regulatory authorities when establishing capital requirements. Since then, VAR has become the established measure of risk exposure in financial services firms.

The most obvious limitation of VAR is that it does not provide a measure of the absolute worst loss. VAR only provides an estimate of losses.

However, there is a 95% probability that a company's loss on a given day, or in a given month, will not exceed a certain amount. VAR is not a useful tool when the management's concern is whether the firm's value will fall below some critical value over an extended period of time. Indeed, VAR has been heavily criticized following the financial crisis of 2007 and was a contributory factor in the downfall of various financial institutions, including Bear Stearns and Lehman Brothers.

On a cautionary note, *New York Times* reporter Joe Nocera wrote an extensive piece, "Risk Mismanagement," on January 4, 2009,[19] discussing the role VAR played in the ongoing financial crisis. After interviewing risk managers, the article suggested that VAR was very useful to risk experts but, nevertheless, exacerbated the crisis by giving false security to bank executives and regulators.

Financial risk management for a nonfinancial corporation is a relatively new concept. To state the problem succinctly, corporate risk is complex. Unlike pure, well-defined financial risks, the risk characteristics of a corporation cannot be easily described by a single equation containing a few variables. Instead, the nonfinancial corporation faces myriad sources of risk. Some classes of risk derive mainly from the underlying operations of the business; for example, competitive risks, business cycle or macroeconomic risks, and technological risks can be classified as business risks. Other classes of risk derive from macroeconomic factors, which include currency risk, interest rate risk, and commodity price risk.

The main issue of relevance to corporations is the predominant focus on cash flows rather than the market values of assets and liabilities. In evaluating their major risks, most nonfinancial companies will want to know how much volatility in their cash flows or firm value an exposure can be expected to cause over periods of at least a year. The VAR approach assumes that the gains and losses from risky positions are "serially independent," which implies that if your firm experiences a loss today, the chance of experiencing another loss tomorrow is unaffected. However, such an assumption is likely to be inappropriate when applied to the operating cash flows of a nonfinancial firm (i.e., if cash flow is poor today, it is more likely to be poor tomorrow). Simulation can be used to build this "serial dependence" of cash flows into an analysis of the probability of financial distress.

As a result of the popularity of VAR for financial institutions, a number of variants have been devised in an attempt to both alleviate some of the problems associated with the original measure and extend its usage beyond the financial services market. We shall briefly review two of these variants and evaluate their potential usefulness for capital budgeting purposes.

Cash Flow at Risk (CFaR)

In contrast to VAR's focus on changes in the overall value of an asset or portfolio as market risk varies, cash flow VAR is instead more focused on operating cash flow during a period and market-induced variations in it that would appear to be of more relevance for capital budgeting. In addition, while VAR tends to involve time periods of relatively short duration (days or weeks), cash flow VAR is calculated over much longer periods (quarters or years). There are basically three steps in implementing a cash flow VAR:

1. The first step consists of delineating business exposures.
2. The next step consists of setting up simulations to model the behavior of key financial variables, commodity prices, exchange rates, and interest rates. The horizon selected needs to match that of the business planning cycle. Note that with longer horizons, the modeling of expected returns is increasingly important, justifying the use of simulation techniques.
3. Finally, these financial variables need to be combined with a business cash flow model. This is akin to attaching a simulation engine to the business cash flow model.

To calculate CFaR, we require a forecast of the probability distribution of cash flow at some future period in time. The dominant method for this is the "bottom-up" approach, which begins with a pro forma cash flow statement and then generates random values for production values and exchange rates. This approach assumes a direct link between production volumes and exchange rates, but it has been suggested that this is too simplistic and only captures a small part of a firm's total risk exposure. From a managerial perspective, the total variability of cash flow is the relevant variable.

Exposure-Based CFaR

Total variability can be attributed to a number of macroeconomic variables (exchange rates, inflation rates, interest rates, etc.), as well as nonmacroeconomic variables and market risk. The calculation of an exposure-based CFaR has been proposed[20] by the following six-step process:

1. Identify relevant macroeconomic and market variables expected to impact corporate performance by a detailed investigation of the firm's competitive environment.
2. Obtain or generate forecasts of the variables identified in point 1.
3. Estimate an exposure model that ideally both is theoretically sound and has good explanatory power.
4. Perform a simulation of the macroeconomic and market variables.
5. Use the simulated values to derive distributions of cash flows to reflect, first, macroeconomic and market variables and, second, all other non-macroeconomic variables that are captured by the error term.
6. Combine the two cash flow distributions into a single distribution and, after deciding on an appropriate confidence level, calculate CFaR.

The authors proceed to describe and discuss in detail the practical application of exposure-based CFaR to an actual company. In closing, they suggest that exposure-based CFaR provides a more transparent view of the portfolio aspects of corporate risk through opportunities to decompose the CFaR estimate into individual risk exposures, which in turn provides a useful insight into both cash flow dynamics and risk drivers.

Conclusion

The completion of this book coincides with a period in time in which the already complex process of making investment decisions is further complicated by ongoing economic and financial circumstances. Although the United States appears to be recovering from the recession, high levels of uncertainty remain regarding the speed of economic recovery and the damage inflicted on the financial institutions, which then, in turn, impact the financial markets. Banks continue to appear reluctant to lend, and equity investors are understandably cautious with such factors impacting both the amount of finance available for capital investment and the cost of such finance. Firms also face additional financial constraints from declining profitability and competing demands for dividend payouts and pension contributions.

In addition, environmental pressures are likely to be a significant factor in the foreseeable future in light of the increasing momentum behind policies to decrease carbon emissions and limit further atmospheric damage. The impact on future modes of transportation and energy supplies is already visible through the development of electric cars and wind farms. Managers will inevitably be confronted with environmental issues in their investment decisions, not only for ethical and social reasons, but also to ensure sustainable economic success. It is likely that environmental, or "green," management will be an integral part of overall corporate strategy and offers opportunities to both reduce costs (relations with stakeholders, costs of materials, and cost of capital) and increase revenues (improved access to certain markets and differentiating products).[1]

Distinctive approaches to both understanding and enhancing investment decision making have been advanced from the disciplines of finance, management accounting, and strategic management. The real options literature attempts to construct a more realistic model of investment decision making by extending the NPV model to include, inter alia, possible deferral of the project as well as future contingent projects. Such strategic options provide an interface between finance and strategic management, though a tension continues to exist between the quantitative focus of finance and the more qualitative insights offered by other disciplines. The complexity of the real options methodology is perhaps a contributory factor in explaining its comparatively low incidence of usage. A further difficulty surrounds the existence of asymmetric information, which implies that managers' preference for short-term success conflicts with the longer term view held by the shareholders. A recent attempt to explain the behavior of managers, investors, and their interactions has been through behavioral finance, which provides a largely qualitative assessment of investment behavior.

The discipline of strategic management has incorporated both reputation and trust as key elements in the investment decision-making process, whereas management accounting, through case study research, identifies the difficulties in applying quantitative approaches when considering corporate strategic goals.

All three disciplines undoubtedly contribute insights to corporate investment and, in some ways, complement each other, although an integrated model of investment behavior seems unlikely as the disciplines diverge in their philosophical viewpoints.

Appendix A

Present Value Table

Present value of 1, e.g. $(1 + r)^{-n}$

Where r = discount rate
n = number of periods until payment

Periods — Discount rates (r)

(n)	1%	2%	3%	4%	5%	6%	7%	8%	9%	10%
1	0.990	0.980	0.971	0.962	0.952	0.943	0.935	0.926	0.917	0.909
2	0.980	0.961	0.943	0.925	0.907	0.890	0.873	0.857	0.842	0.826
3	0.971	0.942	0.915	0.889	0.864	0.840	0.816	0.794	0.772	0.751
4	0.961	0.924	0.888	0.855	0.823	0.792	0.763	0.735	0.708	0.683
5	0.951	0.906	0.863	0.822	0.784	0.747	0.713	0.681	0.650	0.621
6	0.942	0.888	0.837	0.790	0.746	0.705	0.666	0.630	0.596	0.564
7	0.933	0.871	0.813	0.760	0.711	0.665	0.623	0.583	0.547	0.513
8	0.923	0.853	0.789	0.731	0.677	0.627	0.582	0.540	0.502	0.467
9	0.914	0.837	0.766	0.703	0.645	0.592	0.544	0.500	0.460	0.424
10	0.905	0.820	0.744	0.676	0.614	0.558	0.508	0.463	0.422	0.386
11	0.896	0.804	0.722	0.650	0.585	0.527	0.475	0.429	0.388	0.350
12	0.887	0.788	0.701	0.625	0.557	0.497	0.444	0.397	0.356	0.319
13	0.879	0.773	0.681	0.601	0.530	0.469	0.415	0.680	0.326	0.290
14	0.870	0.758	0.661	0.577	0.505	0.442	0.388	0.340	0.299	0.263
15	0.861	0.743	0.642	0.555	0.481	0.417	0.362	0.315	0.275	0.239

(n)	11%	12%	13%	14%	15%	16%	17%	18%	19%	20%
1	0.901	0.893	0.885	0.877	0.870	0.862	0.855	0.847	0.840	0.833
2	0.812	0.797	0.783	0.769	0.756	0.743	0.731	0.718	0.706	0.694
3	0.731	0.712	0.693	0.675	0.658	0.641	0.624	0.609	0.593	0.579
4	0.659	0.636	0.613	0.592	0.572	0.552	0.534	0.516	0.499	0.482
5	0.593	0.567	0.543	0.519	0.497	0.476	0.456	0.437	0.419	0.402
6	0.535	0.507	0.480	0.456	0.432	0.410	0.390	0.370	0.352	0.335
7	0.482	0.452	0.425	0.400	0.376	0.354	0.333	0.314	0.296	0.279
8	0.434	0.404	0.376	0.351	0.327	0.305	0.285	0.266	0.249	0.233
9	0.391	0.361	0.333	0.308	0.284	0.263	0.243	0.225	0.209	0.194
10	0.352	0.322	0.295	0.270	0.247	0.227	0.208	0.191	0.176	0.162
11	0.317	0.287	0.151	0.237	0.215	0.195	0.178	0.162	0.148	0.135
12	0.286	0.257	0.231	0.208	0.187	0.168	0.152	0.137	0.124	0.112
13	0.258	0.229	0.204	0.182	0.163	0.145	0.130	0.116	0.104	0.093
14	0.232	0.205	0.181	0.160	0.141	0.125	0.111	0.099	0.088	0.078
15	0.861	0.183	0.160	0.140	0.123	0.108	0.095	0.084	0.074	0.065

(n)	21%	22%	23%	24%	25%	26%	27%	28%	29%	30%
1	0.826	0.820	0.813	0.807	0.800	0.794	0.787	0.781	0.775	0.799
2	0.683	0.672	0.661	0.650	0.640	0.630	0.620	0.610	0.601	0.592
3	0.565	0.551	0.537	0.525	0.512	0.500	0.488	0.477	0.466	0.455
4	0.467	0.451	0.437	0.423	0.410	0.397	0.384	0.373	0.361	0.350
5	0.386	0.370	0.355	0.341	0.328	0.315	0.303	0.291	0.280	0.269
6	0.319	0.303	0.289	0.275	0.262	0.250	0.238	0.227	0.217	0.207
7	0.263	0.249	0.235	0.222	0.210	0.198	0.188	0.178	0.168	0.159
8	0.218	0.204	0.191	0.179	0.168	0.157	0.148	0.139	0.130	0.123
9	0.180	0.167	0.155	0.144	0.134	0.125	0.116	0.108	0.101	0.094
10	0.149	0.137	0.126	0.116	0.107	0.099	0.092	0.085	0.078	0.073
11	0.123	0.112	0.103	0.094	0.086	0.079	0.072	0.066	0.061	0.056
12	0.102	0.092	0.083	0.076	0.069	0.063	0.057	0.052	0.047	0.043
13	0.084	0.075	0.068	0.061	0.055	0.050	0.045	0.040	0.037	0.033
14	0.069	0.062	0.055	0.049	0.044	0.039	0.035	0.032	0.028	0.025
15	0.057	0.051	0.045	0.040	0.035	0.031	0.028	0.025	0.022	0.020

Appendix B

Annuity Table

Present value of an annuaty of 1, e.g. $\dfrac{1-(1+r)^{-n}}{r}$

Where r = discount rate
n = number of periods

Periods					Discount rates (r)					
(n)	1%	2%	3%	4%	5%	6%	7%	8%	9%	10%
1	0.990	0.980	0.971	0.962	0.952	0.943	0.935	0.926	0.917	0.909
2	1.970	1.942	1.913	1.886	1.859	1.833	1.808	1.783	1.759	1.736
3	2.941	2.884	2.829	2.775	2.723	2.673	2.624	2.577	2.531	2.487
4	3.902	3.808	3.717	3.630	3.546	3.465	3.387	3.312	3.240	3.170
5	4.853	4.713	4.580	4.452	4.329	4.212	4.100	3.993	3.890	3.791
6	5.795	5.601	5.417	5.242	5.076	4.917	4.767	4.623	4.486	4.355
7	6.728	6.472	6.230	6.002	5.786	5.582	5.389	5.206	5.033	4.868
8	7.652	7.325	7.020	6.733	6.463	6.210	5.971	5.747	5.535	5.335
9	8.566	8.162	7.786	7.435	7.108	6.802	6.515	6.247	5.995	5.759
10	9.471	8.983	8.530	8.111	7.722	7.360	7.024	6.710	6.418	6.145
11	10.37	9.787	9.253	8.760	8.306	7.887	7.499	7.139	6.805	6.495
12	11.26	10.58	9.954	9.385	8.863	8.384	7.943	7.536	7.161	6.814
13	12.13	11.35	10.63	9.986	9.394	8.853	8.858	7.904	7.487	7.103
14	13.00	12.11	11.30	10.56	9.899	9.295	8.745	8.244	7.786	7.367
15	13.87	12.85	11.94	11.12	10.38	9.712	9.108	8.559	8.061	7.606

	11%	12%	13%	14%	15%	16%	17%	18%	19%	20%
1	0.901	0.893	0.885	0.877	0.870	0.862	0.855	0.847	0.840	0.833
2	1.713	1.690	1.668	1.647	1.626	1.605	1.585	1.566	1.547	1.528
3	2.444	2.402	2.361	2.322	2.283	2.246	2.210	2.174	2.140	2.106
4	3.102	3.037	2.974	2.914	2.855	2.798	2.743	2.690	2.639	2.589
5	3.696	3.605	3.517	3.433	3.352	3.274	3.199	3.127	3.058	2.991
6	4.231	4.111	3.998	3.889	3.784	3.685	3.589	3.498	3.410	3.326
7	4.712	4.564	4.423	4.288	4.160	4.039	3.922	3.812	3.706	3.605
8	5.146	4.968	4.799	4.639	4.487	4.344	4.207	4.078	20954	3.837
9	5.537	5.328	5.132	4.946	4.772	4.608	4.451	4.303	4.163	4.031
10	5.889	5.650	5.426	5.216	5.019	4.833	4.659	4.494	4.339	4.192
11	6.207	5.938	5.687	5.453	5.234	5.029	4.836	4.656	4.486	4.327
12	6.492	6.194	5.918	5.660	5.421	5.197	4.988	4.793	4.611	4.439
13	6.750	6.424	6.122	5.842	5.583	5.342	5.118	4.910	4.715	4.533
14	6.982	6.628	6.302	6.002	5.724	5.468	5.229	5.008	4.802	4.611
15	7.191	6.811	6.462	6.142	5.847	5.575	5.324	5.092	4.876	4.675

	21%	22%	23%	24%	25%	26%	27%	28%	29%	30%
1	0.826	0.820	0.813	0.806	0.800	0.794	0.787	0.781	0.775	0.769
2	1.509	1.492	1.474	1.457	1.440	1.424	1.407	0.610	1.376	1.361
3	2.074	2.042	2.011	1.981	1.952	1.923	1.896	0.477	1.842	1.816
4	2.540	2.494	2.448	2.404	2.362	2.320	2.280	0.373	2.203	2.166
5	2.926	2.864	2.803	2.745	2.689	2.635	2.583	0.291	2.483	2.436
6	3.245	3.167	3.092	3.020	2.951	2.885	2.821	0.227	2.700	2.643
7	3.508	3.416	3.327	3.242	3.161	3.083	3.009	0.178	2.868	2.802
8	3.726	3.619	3.518	3.421	3.329	3.241	3.156	0.139	2.999	2.925
9	3.905	3.786	3.673	3.566	3.463	3.366	3.273	0.108	3.100	3.019
10	4.054	3.923	3.799	3.682	3.571	3.465	3.364	0.085	3.178	3.092
11	4.177	4.035	3.902	3.776	3.656	3.543	3.437	0.066	3.239	3.147
12	5.278	4.127	3.985	3.851	3.725	3.606	3.493	0.052	3.286	3.190
13	4.362	4.203	4.053	3.912	3.780	3.656	3.538	0.040	3.322	3.223
14	4.432	4.265	4.108	3.962	3.824	3.695	3.573	0.032	3.351	3.249
15	4.489	4.315	4.153	4.001	3.859	3.726	3.601	0.025	3.373	3.268

Notes

Introduction

1. Dow Jones (May 2009).
2. Taylor (2009).
3. Anglo American (2008).
4. Metal Bulletin Research (December 2008).
5. Reuters (July 27, 2009).

Chapter 1

1. United Nations (2009).
2. *Financial Times* (2009).
3. Jensen and Meckling (1976).
4. Myers and Majluf (1984).
5. Miller and Modigliani (1961).
6. Gatchev, Spindt, and Tarhan (2009).

Chapter 2

1. Robinson and Schroeder (2004).
2. Burns and Walker (2009).
3. Gordon and Pinches (1984); Mukherjee (1987).
4. Gordon and Pinches (1984).

Chapter 3

1. Miller and Modigliani (1961).
2. Graham and Harvey (2001) in the United States; Pike (1996) and Arnold and Hatzopoulos (2000) in the United Kingdom; Brounen, de Jong, and Koedijk (2004) in Europe.
3. Graham and Harvey (2001); Ryan and Ryan (2002).
4. Gitman and Forrester (1977).
5. Pike (1996).
6. Arnold and Hatzopoulos (2000).

7. Alkaran and Northcott (2006).

8. Brounen, de Jong, and Koedijk (2004).

9. Truong, Partington, and Peat (2008).

10. Cohen and Yagil (2007).

11. Truong, Partington, and Peat (2008).

12. Pike and Ooi (1988).

13. Pike and Neale (1999).

14. Grinyer and Green (2003).

Chapter 4

1. Drury and Thayles (1997).

2. Graham and Harvey (2001).

3. Bruner, Eades, Harris, and Higgins (1998).

4. Gitman and Mercurio (1982); Gitman and Vandenburg (2000).

5. McLaney, Pointon, Thomas, and Tucker (2004).

6. Brounen, de Jong, and Koeddijk (2004).

7. Payne, Heath, and Gale (1999).

8. McLaney et al. (2004).

9. Poterba and Summers (1995).

10. Ross (1986).

11. Driver and Temple (2009).

Chapter 5

1. AT&T (2009).

2. Bierman (1986).

3. Klammer and Walker (1984).

4. Pike (1988).

5. Ho and Pike (1991).

6. Alkaran and Northcott (2006); Arnold and Hatzopoulos (2000).

Chapter 6

1. Fremgen (1973); Gitman and Forrester (1977).

2. Mukherjee and Hingorani (1999).

3. Campello, Graham, and Harvey (2009).

Chapter 7

1. IAS Plus (2003).
2. Equipment Leasing and Finance Association (2009).
3. Finance and Leasing Association (2009).

Chapter 8

1. Harris, Emmanuel, and Komakech (2009).
2. Kaplan and Norton (1992).
3. Gregory (1995).
4. Roussel et al. (1991).
5. Groenveld (1997), p. 48.
6. Phaal, Farrukh, and Probert (2004).
7. Garcia and Bray (1997).
8. Miller and O'Leary (2007).
9. Porter (1985).
10. Shank and Govindarajan (1992).
11. Crain and Abraham (2008).
12. Shank and Govindarajan (1992).
13. Hoque (2001).
14. Hoque (2001).
15. Camp (1989).
16. Mayle et al. (2002).
17. Putterill et al. (1996).
18. Carr and Tomkins (1996).
19. Alkaraan and Northcott (2006).

Chapter 9

1. Eiteman and Stonehill (2010).
2. Block (2000).
3. Holmen and Pramborg (2009).

Chapter 10

1. Dixit and Pindyck (1994).
2. Copeland and Weiner (1990).
3. Luehrman (1988).
4. Lewent (1994).
5. Trigeorgis (1996).

6. Broyles (2003).
7. Busby and Pitts (1998).
8. Cottrell and Sick (2001).
9. Copeland and Antikarov (2001).
10. Busby and Pitts (1997).
11. Buckley, Buckley, Langevin, and Tse (1996).
12. Triantis and Borison (2001).
13. Ryan and Ryan (2002); Teach (2003).
14. Block (2007).
15. Macauley (1938).
16. Arnold and North (2008).
17. Ray (2008).
18. Andren, Jankensgard, and Oxelheim (2005); Suroweicki (2004).
19. Nocera (2009).
20. Ambec and Lanoie (2008).

Conclusion

1. Ambec and Lanoie (2008).

References

Alkaraan, F., & Northcott, D. (2006). Strategic capital investment decision-making: A role for emergent analysis tools? A study of practice in large UK manufacturing companies. *British Accounting Review, 38,* 149–173.

Ambec, S., & Lanoie, P. (2008). Does it pay to be green? A systematic overview. *Academy of Management Perspectives, 22*(6), 45–62.

Andren, N., Jankensgard, H., & Oxelheim, L. (2005). Exposure-based cash-flow-at-risk: An alternative to VaR for industrial companies. *Journal of Applied Corporate Finance, 17*(3), 76–86.

Anglo American. (2008, December 17). Anglo American reduces 2009 capital expenditure by more than $50 to $4.5 billion. [Press release]. Retrieved from http://www.angloamerican.co.uk/aa/media/releases/2008pr/2008-12-17

Arnold, G. C., & Hatzopoulos, P. D. (2000). The theory-practice gap in capital budgeting: Evidence from the United Kingdom. *Journal of Business Finance and Accounting, 27* (5 & 6), 603–626.

Arnold, T., & North, D. S. (2008). Duration Measures for corporate project valuation. *The Engineering Economist, 53,* 103–117.

AT&T. (2009). *Road to growth study: U.S. perspectives on information technology.* Retrieved from http://www.att.com/gen/press-room?pid=239

Bierman, H. (1986). *Implementation of Capital Budgeting Techniques: Survey and Synthesis.* Tampa, FL: Financial Management Association.

Block, S. (2000). Integrating traditional capital budgeting concepts into an international decision-making environment. *The Engineering Economist, 45*(4), 309–324.

Block, S. (2007). Are "real options" actually used in the real world? *The Engineering Economist, 52*(3), 255–268.

Brounen, D., de Jong, A., & Koedijk, K. (2004). Corporate finance in Europe: Confronting theory with practice. *Financial Management, 33*(4), 71–101.

Broyles, J. (2003). *Financial Management and Real Options.* Chichester, England: John Wiley & Sons.

Bruner, R. F., Eades, K. M., Harris, R., & Higgins, R. C. (1998). Best practices in estimating the cost of capital: Survey and synthesis. *Financial Practice and Education, 8,* 13–28.

Buckley, A., Buckley, P., Langevin, P., & Tse, K. L. (1996). The financial analysis of foreign investment decisions by large UK-based companies. *European Journal of Finance, 2*(2), 181–206.

Burns, R. M., & Walker, J. (1997). Capital budgeting techniques among the Fortune 500: A rationale approach. *Managerial Finance, 23*(9), 3–15.

Burns, R. M., & Walker, J. (2009). Capital budgeting surveys: The future is now. *Journal of Applied Corporate Finance, 19*(1/2), 78–90.

Busby, J. S., & Pitts, C. G. (1997). Real options in practice: An exploratory survey of how finance officers deal with flexibility in capital appraisal. *Management Accounting Research, 8,* 169–186.

Busby, J. S., & Pitts, C. G. (1998). *Assessing Flexibility in Capital Investment.* London, England: The Chartered Institute of Management Accountants.

Camp, R. C. (1989). *Benchmarking: The Search for Industry Best Practices That Lead to Superior Performance.* Milwaukee, WI: ASQC Quality.

Campello, M., Graham, J., & Harvey, C. R. (2010). The real effects of financial constraints: Evidence from a financial crisis. *Journal of Financial Economics, 97*(3), 470–487.

Carr, C., & Tomkins, C. (1996). Strategic investment decisions: The importance of SCM. *Management Accounting Research, 7*(2), 199–217.

Cohen, G., & Yagil, Y. (2007). A multinational survey of corporate financial policies. *Journal of Applied Finance, 17*(1), 57–69.

Copeland, T., & Antikarov, V. (2001). *Real Options: A Practitioner's Guide.* New York, NY: Texere.

Copeland, T., & Weiner, J. (1990). Proactive management of uncertainty. *The McKinsey Quarterly, 10*(4), 133–152.

Cottrell, T., & Sick, G. (2001). First mover (dis)advantage and real options. *Journal of Applied Corporate Finance, 14*(2), 41–51.

Crain, D. W., & Abraham, S. (2008). Using value-chain analysis to discover customers' strategic needs. *Strategy and Leadership, 36*(4), 29–39.

Dixit, A., & Pindyck, R. S. (1994). *Investment Under Uncertainty.* Princeton, NJ: Princeton University Press.

Dow Jones. (2009). Toyota slashes capital spending, R&D spending amid losses. May 8.

Driver, C., & Temple, P. (2009). Why do hurdle rates differ from the cost of capital? *Cambridge Journal of Economics, 34,* 501–523.

Drury, C., & Tayles, M. (1997). Evidence on the financial accounting debate: A research note. *British Accounting Review, 29*(3), 263–276.

Eiteman, D. K., Stonehill, A. I., & Moffett, M. H. (2010). *Multinational Business Finance,* 12th ed. Boston, MA: Prentice Hall.

Equipment Leasing and Finance Association. (2009, November). *Survey of Economic Activity,* http://www.elfaonline.org

Finance and Leasing Association. (2009, September). FLA newsletter update. Retrieved from http://www.fla.org.uk/media

Financial Times. (2009). Welcome to a world of low predictability. Retrieved from http://media.ft.com/cms/71ae4d84-3404-11de-9eea-00144feabdc0.pdf

Fremgen, J. (1973, May). Capital budgeting practices: A survey. *Management Accounting, 54*, 19–25.

Garcia, M. L., & Bray, O. H. (1997). *Fundamentals of Technology Roadmapping.* Strategic Business Development Department, Sandia National Laboratories. Retrieved from http://www.sandia.gov/Roadmap/home.htm.what02

Gatchev, V. A., Spindt, P., & Tarhan, V. (2009). How do firms finance their investments? The relative importance of equity issuance and debt contracting costs. *Journal of Corporate Finance, 15*(2), 179–195.

Gitman, L. J., & Forrester, J. R. (1977). A survey of capital budgeting techniques used by major U.S. firms. *Financial Management, 6*(3), 66–71.

Gitman, L. J., & Mercurio, V. A. (1982). Cost of capital techniques used by major US firms: Survey and analysis of Fortune's 1000. *Financial Management, 11*(4), 21–29.

Gitman, L. J., & Vandenberg, P. A. (2000). Cost of capital techniques used by major US firms: 1997 v 1980. *Financial Practice and Education, 10*(2), 53–68.

Gordon, L. A., & Pinches, G. E. (1984). *Improving Capital Budgeting: A Decision Support System Approach.* Reading, MA: Addison-Wesley.

Graham, J. R., & Harvey, C. R. (2001). The theory and practice of corporate finance: Evidence from the field. *Journal of Financial Economics, 60*(2/3), 187–243.

Gregory, M. J. (1995). Technology management: A process approach. *Proceedings of the Institute of Mechanical Engineers, 209*, 347–356.

Grinyer, J. R., & Green, C. D. (2003). Managerial advantages of using payback as a surrogate for NPV. *The Engineering Economist, 48*(2),152–168.

Groenveld, P. (1997). Road-mapping integrates business and technology. *Research Technology Management, 40*(5), 48–55.

Harris, E. P., Emmanuel, C. R., & Komakech, S. (2009). *From Managerial Judgement and Strategic Investment Decisions.* Oxford, England: CIMA.

Ho, S., & Pike, R. H. (1991). Risk analysis in capital budgeting contexts: Simple or sophisticated? *Accounting and Business Research, 21*(83), 227–238.

Holman, M., & Pramborg, B. (2009). Capital budgeting and political risk: Empirical evidence. *Journal of International Financial Management and Accounting, 20*(2), 105–134.

Hoque, Z. (2001). *Strategic Management Accounting: Concepts, Procedures and Issues.* Oxford, England: Chandos.

IAS Plus. (2003). IASB IAS17 leases summary. Retrieved from http://www.iasplus.com/standard/ias17.htm

Jensen, M. C., & Meckling, W. H. (1976, October). Theory of the firm: Managerial behavior, agency costs and ownership structure. *Journal of Financial Economics, 3*(4), 305–360.

Kaplan, R. S., & Norton, D. P. (1992, January–February). The balanced scorecard: Measures that drive performance. *Harvard Business Review, 70*(1), 71–79.

Klammer, T. P., & Walker, M. C. (1984, Fall). The continuing increase in the use of sophisticated capital budgeting techniques. *California Management Review, 27*(1), 137–148.

Lewent, J. (1994, January–February). Scientific management at Merck: An interview with CFO Judy Lewent. *Harvard Business Review 72*(1), 89–105.

Luehrman, T. A. (1998). Strategy as a portfolio of real options. *Harvard Business Review, 76*(5), 89–99.

Macauley, F. (1938). *The Movements of Interest Rates, Bond Yields and Stock Prices in the United States Since 1856*. New York, NY: National Bureau of Economic Research.

Mayle, D., Hinton, M., Francis, G., & Holloway, J. (2002). What really goes on in the name of benchmarking? In A. Neely (Ed.), *Business Performance Measurement: Theory and Practice* (pp. 211–225). Cambridge, England: Cambridge University Press.

McLaney, E., Pointon, J., Thomas, M., & Tucker, J. (2004). Practitioners' perspectives on the UK cost of capital. *European Journal of Finance, 10*, 123–138.

Metal Bulletin Research. (2008, December). Capex cuts threatens projects on the pipeline: Supply analysis.

Miller, M. H., & Modigliani, F. (1961). Dividend policy, growth and the valuation of shares. *Journal of Business, 34*, 411–433.

Miller, P., & O'Leary, T. (2007). Flexibility, complementarity relations and mechanisms of investment appraisal. In L. Trigeorgis (Ed.), *Innovation, Organisation and Strategy* (pp. 234–278). Oxford, England: Oxford University Press.

Mukherjee, T. K. (1987, Spring). Capital budgeting surveys: The past and the future. *Review of Business and Economic Research, 22*(2), 37–56.

Mukherjee, T. K., & Hingorani, V. L. (1999). Capital-rationing decisions of Fortune 500 firms: A survey. *Financial Practice and Education, 9*(1), 7–15.

Myers, S., & Majluf, N. S. (1984). Corporate financing and investment decisions when firms have information that investors do not have. *Journal of Financial Economics, 13*(2), 187–221.

Nocera, J. (2009, January 2). Risk mismanagement. *The New York Times*. Retrieved from http://www.nytimes.com/2009/01/04/magazine/04risk-t.html?_r=3

Payne, J., Heath W., & Gale, L. (1999). Comparative financial practice in the US and Canada: Capital budgeting and risk assessment techniques. *Financial Practice and Education, 9,* 16–24.

Phaal, R., Farrukh, C. J. P., & Probert, D. R. (2004). Customising roadmapping. *Research Technology Management, 47,* 26–37.

Pike, R. H. (1988). An empirical study of the adoption of sophisticated capital budgeting practices and decision-making effectiveness. *Accounting and Business Research, 18*(72), 341–351.

Pike, R. H. (1996). A longitudinal survey on capital budgeting practices. *Journal of Business Finance and Accounting, 23*(1), 79–92.

Pike, R. H., & Neale, B. (1999). *Corporate Finance and Investment* (3rd ed.). Harlow, England: Prentice Hall.

Pike, R. H., & Ooi, T. S. (1988). The impact of corporate investment objectives and constraints on capital budgeting practice. *British Accounting Review, 20*(2), 159–173.

Porter, M. E. (1985). *Competitive Advantage: Creating and Sustaining Superior Performance.* New York, NY: Free Press.

Poterba, J. M., & Summers, L. H. (1995). A CEO survey of U.S. companies' time horizons and hurdle rates. *Sloan Management Review, 37*(1), 43–53.

Putterill, M., Maguire, W., & Sohal, A. (1996). Advanced manufacturing technology investment: Criteria for organisational choice and appraisal. *Integrated Manufacturing Systems, 7*(5), 12–24.

Ray, R. (2008). Decision markets: A powerful capital-budgeting tool. *Corporate Finance Review, 13*(1), 5–9.

Reuters. (2009). News release. July 27 2009.

Robinson, A., & Schroeder, D. M. (2004). *Ideas Are Free: How the Idea Revolution Is Liberating People and Transforming Organisations.* San Francisco, CA: Berrett Koehler.

Ross, M. (1986, Winter). Capital budgeting practices of twelve large manufacturers. *Financial Management, 15,* 15–22.

Roussel, P. A., Saad, K. N., & Erickson, T. J. (1991). *Third Generation R&D— Managing the Link to Corporate Strategy.* Boston, MA: Harvard Business University Press.

Ryan, P. A., & Ryan, G. P. (2002). Capital budgeting practices of the Fortune 1000: How have things changed? *Journal of Business and Management, 8*(4), 355–364.

Shank, J. K., & Govindarajan, V. (1992). Strategic cost management: The value chain perspective. *Journal of Management Accounting Research, 4,* 179–197.

Suroweicki, J. (2004). *The Wisdom of Crowds.* London, England: Abacus.

Taylor, P. (2009, January 29). AT&T to slash capital spending. *Financial Times.* Retrieved from http://www.ft.com/cms/s/0/5c450f26-eda7-11dd-bd60-00 00779fd2ac.html

Teach, E. (2003, July). Will real options take root? *CFO Magazine.* Retrieved from http://www.cfo.com/article.cfm/3009782/c_3046594?f=magazine_alsoinside

Triantis, A., & Borison, A. (2001). Real options: State of the practice. *Journal of Applied Corporate Finance, 14*(2), 8–24.

Trigeorgis, L. (1996). *Real Options: Managerial Flexibility and Strategy in Resource Allocation.* Cambridge, MA: MIT Press.

Truong, G. L., Partington, G., & Peat, M. (2008). Cost of capital estimation and capital budgeting practice in Australia. *Australian Journal of Management, 33*(1), 95–121.

United Nations. (2009). World economic situation and prospects. Retrieved from http://www.un.org/esa/policy/wess/wesp2009files/wesp2009.pdf.

Index